D1806536

To my dear wife,
ALICE MARY,

I dedicate this book,
in token of my appreciation of her gentle and
tender kindness towards all animal life,
more particularly "The cat."

"Iddesleigh," Sevenoaks.
March 12th 1889

CONTENTS

12|4

OUR CATS
and
ALL ABOUT THEM

Their Varieties,
Habits, and Management;
And for Show,

The Standard of
Excellence and Beauty;
Described and Pictured

By

HARRISON WEIR

First published in 1889

This edition published by Read Books Ltd.
Copyright © 2019 Read Books Ltd.
This book is copyright and may not be
reproduced or copied in any way without
the express permission of the publisher in writing

British Library Cataloguing-in-Publication Data
A catalogue record for this book is available
from the British Library

ILLUSTRATIONS

CATS

The domestic cat (*Felis Catus* or *Felis Silvestris Catus*) is a small, usually furry, domesticated, and carnivorous mammal – the most popular pet in the world. They are valued and kept by humans for companionship, their ability to hunt vermin, as well as a general household and farmyard pet.

Since cats were cult animals in ancient Egypt (associated with the goddesses Isis and Ba'at), they were commonly believed to have been domesticated there. Despite this common belief, there may have been instances of domestication as early as the Neolithic period. Cats were originally domesticated because they hunted mice that would eat stored grains, protecting the food stores. It was a beneficial situation for both species: cats got a reliable source of prey, and humans got effortless pest control. This mutually beneficial arrangement began the relationship between cats and humans which continues to this day.

While the exact history of human interaction with cats is still somewhat vague, a shallow grave site discovered in 1983 in Cyprus, dating to 7500 BCE, during the Neolithic period, contains the skeleton of a human, buried ceremonially with stone tools, a lump of iron oxide, and a handful of seashells. In its own tiny grave, forty centimetres from the human grave was an eight-month-old cat, its body oriented in the same westward direction as the human skeleton. Cats are not native to Cyprus, thus providing evidence that cats were being tamed just as humankind was establishing the first settlements in the part of the Middle East known as the Fertile Crescent.

A genetic study in 2007 concluded that domestic cats are descended from African wildcats, having diverged around 8000 BCE in West Asia. Within this family of domestic cats, there are seven sub-species (depending upon classification scheme).

Members of the genus are found worldwide and include the jungle cat (*Felis chaus*) of southeast Asia, European wildcat (*F. silvestris silvestris*), African wildcat (*F. s. lybica*), the Chinese mountain cat (*F. bieti*), and the Arabian sand cat (*F. margarita*), among others. The domestic cat was first classified as *Felis catus* by Carolus Linnaeus in the tenth edition of his *Systema Naturae* in 1758.

Cats are similar in anatomy to the other felids, with strong, flexible bodies, quick reflexes, sharp retractable claws, and teeth adapted to killing small prey. Their senses fit an ecological niche, able to hear sounds too faint or high for human ears, such as those made by mice and other small animals. Cats can also seen in near darkness, and like most other mammals have poorer colour vision and a better sense of smell than humans. Despite being solitary hunters, cats are a very social species, and their communication includes a variety of mewing, purring, trilling, hissing, growling and grunting, as well as pheromones and body language.

In terms of domestic care, having a cat neutered can confer significant health benefits. This is because castrated males cannot develop testicular cancer, spayed females cannot develop uterine or ovarian cancer, and both have a reduced risk of mammary cancer. Cats also have a high breeding rate, and under controlled breeding, can be bred and shown as registered pedigree pets – a hobby known as 'cat fancy'. Failure to control the breeding of pet cats by neutering, and the abandonment of former household pets, has resulted in large numbers of feral cats however, sadly necessitating population control measures worldwide.

In comparison to dogs, cats have not undergone major changes during the domestication process, as the form and behaviour of the domestic cat is not radically different from those of wildcats and domestic cats. Fully domesticated house cats often interbreed with feral populations, meaning that hybridisation can occur with many other felids (most notably the Asian leopard cat). Several natural behaviours and characteristics of wildcats may have pre-adapted them for domestication as pets. These traits include their small size, social nature, obvious body language, love of play and relatively high intelligence; they may also have an inborn tendency towards tameness.

The cultural depiction of cats and their relationship to humans is as old as civilization itself, and stretches back over 9,500 years. Cats have figured in the history of many nations, are the subject of legend and a favourite focus of artists and writers. In Norse mythology, the goddess Freyja (connected with love, sexuality, beauty, fertility, gold, war, and death) was associated with cats. Farmers sought protection for their crops by leaving pans of milk in their fields for Freya's feline companions – the two grey cats who fought with her and pulled her chariot.

Despite their usefulness and widespread domestication, cats have had a mixed reputation throughout history. European folklore dating back to as early as 1607 tells that a cat will suffocate a newborn infant by putting its nose to the child's mouth, sucking the breath out of the infant. Cats were also associated with witches, and were killed *en masse* in the middle of the fourteenth century during the time of the Black Death. Ironically, had this bias toward cats not existed, local rodent populations could have been kept down, lessening the spread of plague-infected fleas from host to host.

The association with cats and witches continued into the renaissance period. Yet as we move towards the age of enlightenment, these dark associations shifted and cats became popular and sympathetic characters in such folk tales as *Puss in Boots* and *Dick Whittington*. They have a much better reputation in Japanese culture, where there is the 'Maneki Neko', a 'good luck' cat. It usually sits with a paw raised and bent, as legend has it that a Japanese landlord who was once intrigued by this gesture, went towards it. A few seconds later a lightning bolt struck where the landlord had been previously standing, and he attributed his luck to the friendly cat. Cats have also been considered good luck in Russia for centuries. Owning a cat, and especially letting one into a new house before the humans move in, is said to bring good fortune.

In yet more superstitions, black cats are generally held to be unlucky in the United States and Europe, and to portend good luck in the United Kingdom. In the U.K, a black cat entering a house or ship is a good omen, and a sailor's wife should have a black cat for her husband's safety on the sea. Elsewhere, it is unlucky if a black cat crosses one's path; as black cats have been associated with death and darkness. White cats, bearing the colour of ghosts, are conversely held to be unlucky in the United Kingdom, while tortoiseshell cats are lucky.

Cats are common pets in Europe and North America, and today, their worldwide population exceeds 500 million. They are a fascinating species, and domestic cats have proved to be invaluable as well as comforting companions to humans throughout the ages. Cat owners as well as scholars, veterinarians and anatomists all over the world are incredibly passionate about their breeding and care, and it is hoped that the current reader enjoys this book about cats.

PREFACE

"What is aught, but as 'tis valued?"

Troilus and Cressida, Act II.

The following notes and illustrations of and respecting the Cat are the outcome of over fifty years' careful, thoughtful, heedful observation, much research, and not unprofitable attention to the facts and fancies of others. From a tiny child to the present, the love of Nature has been my chief delight; animals and birds have not only been objects of study, but of deep and absorbing interest. I have noted their habits, watched their ways, and found lasting pleasure in their companionship. This love of animal life and Nature, with all its moods and phases, has grown with me from childhood to manhood, and is not the least enjoyable part of my old age.

Among animals possibly the most perfect, and certainly the most domestic, is the Cat. I did not think so always, having had a bias against it, and was some time coming to this belief; nevertheless, such is the fact. It is a veritable part of our household, and is both useful, quiet, affectionate, and ornamental. The small or large dog may be regarded and petted, but is generally *useless*; the Cat, a pet or not, *is of service*. Were it not for our Cats, rats and mice would overrun our house, buildings, cultivated and other lands. If there were not *millions* of Cats, there would be *billions* of vermin.

Long ages of neglect, ill-treatment, and absolute cruelty, with little or no gentleness, kindness, or training, have made the Cat self-reliant; and from this emanates the marvellous powers of observation, the concentration of which has produced a state analogous to reasoning, not unmixed with timidity, caution, wildness, and a retaliative nature.

But should a new order of things arise, and it is nurtured, petted, cosseted, talked to, noticed, and *trained*, with mellowed firmness and tender gentleness, then in but a few generations much evil that bygone cruelty has stamped into its often wretched existence will disappear, and it will be more than ever not only a useful, serviceable helpmate, but an object of increasing interest, admiration, and cultured beauty, and, thus being of value, profitable.

Having said this much, I turn to the pleasurable duty of recording my deep sense of the kindness of those warm-hearted friends who have assisted me in "my labour of love," not the least among these being those publishers, who, with a generous and prompt alacrity, gave me permission to make extracts, excerpts, notes, and quotations from the following high-class works, their property. My best thanks are due to Messrs. Longmans & Co., Blaine's "Encyclopædia of British Sports;" Allen & Co., Rev. J. F. Thiselton Dyer's "English Folk-lore;" Cassell & Company (Limited), Dr. Brewer's "Dictionary of Phrase and Fable," and "Old and New London;" Messrs. Chatto & Windus, "History of Sign-boards;" Mr. J. Murray, Jamieson's "Scottish Dictionary," and others. I am also indebted to Messrs. Walker & Boutal, and The Phototype Company, for the able manner in which they have rendered my drawings; and for the careful printing, to my good friends Messrs. Charles Dickens & Evans.

Harrison Weir.
"Iddesleigh," Sevenoaks,
May 5th, 1889.

PREFACE TO NEW EDITION

"'Twas pitiful, 'twas wondrous pitiful."

Othello.

Some time has passed since I published my book, "Our Cats and all about them," in 1889, and much has taken place regarding these household pets. All know as well as myself that each and everything about us changes, nothing stands still; that which is of to-day is past, and that which was hidden often revealed, sometimes by mere accident, at others by scientific research; but one was scarcely prepared in any way for so wonderful "a find" as that of the large number of "mummy" Cats at Beni Hassan, Central Egypt. They were discovered by an Egyptian fellah, employed in husbandry, who tumbled into a pit which, on further examination, proved to be a large subterranean cave completely filled with mummy Cats, every one of which had been separately embalmed and wrapped in cloth, after the manner of the Egyptian human mummies, all being laid out carefully in rows; and here they had lain probably about three or four thousand years. The "totem" of a section of the ancients, as is well known, was the Cat; hence when a Cat died it was buried with due honours, being embalmed, and often decorated in various ways, and, in short, had as much attention paid to it as a human being. It had long been believed that a Cat cemetery existed on the east bank of the Nile, and in the autumn of 1889 the lucky Egyptian, about 100 miles from Cairo, came unexpectedly upon it.

Immediately on "the find" becoming known, "specimen" mummy Cats were written for to agents in Egypt, one friend of

17

mine sending for four, and it appeared for a while that much money would be realised by the owner of the cave or land in this way; but the number was too great, and the prices and the interest gave way, and, sad to relate, these former "Deities" were dug out of their resting-place by hundreds of thousands, and quickly sold to local farmers, being used for enriching the land. Other lots found their way to an Alexandrian merchant, and were by him sent to Liverpool on board the steamer *Pharos and Thebes*.

The consignment consisted of 19½ tons, and were sold by auction, mostly being bought by a local "fertiliser" merchant. The auction was only known to the trade, and the lots were "knocked down" at the "giving away" sums of £3 13s.9d., £3 17s., to £4 5s. *per ton*, the big and the perfect ones being picked out for the museum and private collections. The broker who sold used a head of one of these Cats in lieu of an auctioneer's hammer. And now these tons of "deified" Cats are used for manure, and in our English soil plants grow into them, and on them, and of them; and, if it be true, as chemists assert, these plants take into their system that on which they feed, and so, if so, possibly in our very bread that we have eaten, we have swallowed "*a little* at a time part of if not the whole of a deified cat."

I made several endeavours to find out from those on the spot at Liverpool whether there was any hair of colours in existence among the mass of bodies; but in no case could I succeed in getting any, as I had hoped by this means to possibly come to some conclusion as to the kind or breed. Of course, it is well known from mummies long in this country what form, size, and general appearance the Egyptian possessed; but as yet, as far as I can learn, no one has found so much, if any, of the fur as to be able to determine the colour.

Apropos with the above, as applying the bodies of the mummy Cats for manure, comes the modern idea of keeping Cats for their fur. It is stated that a company has been formed in America for that purpose in Washington, and an island of some size has been bought or leased for the purpose. The intention is to raise entirely black Cats; and as their place of abode will be surrounded by water, it is conjectured that after the first importation they will go on propagating and producing only Cats of that beautiful though sombre dark hue. The Cats with which the island is to be stocked are to be procured from Holland, where already the "industry" is "at work." So much so that a friend of mine, an elderly gentleman, sending to a furrier in Holland to know what kind of fur he would recommend as the best for warmth, received the reply that Cats' skins "were the most useful and warmest." A few days ago he called on me wrapped in a cloth coat, with fur collar and cuffs, and *lining throughout of black Cats' skins*, and I am bound to say that the general appearance was much in its favour; he also stated that he was in every way perfectly satisfied.

By-the-bye, the Cat Company intend to feed their Cats on fish, which abound about the shores of their island, and so they affirm the food will cost nothing, and their profits consequently be very large. But in this I hope they have been well informed as to the adaptability of the Cat to feed *entirely* on fish, for of this I have my doubts; certainly those I have had did not appear to thrive if they had fish too often.

Again, as the Cats are to roam the island at their "own sweet will," I take it there will be at times some "damaging of fur" by the playful way in which they so often engage, when jealousy incites them to mortal combat. But possibly this has been considered and duly entered in the "profit and loss" account.

While writing that portion of my book in which I referred to the superstitions connected with the domestic Cat, and the amazing stories told of the witches' Cats, I felt convinced that in those darkened and foolish times that the very fact of the wonderful faculty the Cat possesses of applying what it observes to its own purposes was in some way the cause of the ignorant and superstitious considering that it was "possessed" of an evil spirit. I therefore searched for proofs among the evidence given at the trial of witches, and was, as I expected, rewarded for my trouble. What a Cat would do now would not unreasonably be thought clever and showing much sagacity, if not attributes of a deeper kind.

Yet I find that at a trial for witchcraft, the following questions were put to a man: "Well! and what did you see?" "Well! I saw her Cat walk up and try to open the door by the latch." "What did you do?" "I immediately killed it." This, which is now regarded as an everyday example of the intelligence of the Cat, bore hardly in the evidence against the witch. Sir Walter Scott, in his letter on "Demonology and Witchcraft," tells of "a poor old woman condemned, as usual, on her own confession, and on the testimony of a neighbour, who deposed that he saw a Cat jump in the accused person's cottage through the window at twilight, one evening, and that he verily believed the Cat to be the devil, on which precious testimony the poor wretch was hanged." One more note and I leave the subject. A certain carpenter, named William Montgomery, was so infested with Cats, which, as his servant-maid reported, "spoke among themselves," that he fell in a rage upon a party of these animals, which had assembled in his house at irregular hours, and betwixt his Highland arms of knife, dirk, and broadsword, and his professional weapon of an axe, he made such a dispersion that they were quiet for the night. In consequence of his blows *two witches* are said to have died.

Since writing of the English wild Cat, I had the pleasure of meeting Mr. Francis Darwin (brother of Mr. Charles Darwin) on board the steamboat going to St. Servan, when, in the course of conversation, he informed me that a wild Cat was killed at Bramhope Moor Plantation, in 1841, a keeper having caught it in *two* traps.

In February of this year, 1891, my kind friend, Mr. Dresser, of Orpington, the well-known naturalist, wrote to me to know whether I would like to have a kitten half-bred between the British Wild Cat and a domestic she Cat, which I was unfortunately obliged to decline, fearing it would "make matters unpleasant" with what I had. He very kindly supplied me with the following particulars forwarded to him by O. H. Mactheyer, Esq.: "Mr.

Harrison Weir can see the papa of the kitten at the Zoo.

"He is a young Cat (under a year old, we thought, by the teeth). He was seen one moonlight night in company with my 'stalker's' small lean black Cat, right away in my deer forest. We caught the papa in a trap after he had killed a number of grouse, and not being badly hurt, I sent him to Bartlett at the Zoo. We are thoroughly up to real wild Cats here. I have caught them forty-three inches from nose to tail-end; tails as thick at the point as at the root; the ears are also differently set on. Martin Cats, Polecats, and Badgers are all extinct here, and it is ten years since we got the last wild Cat, but three have been killed in this district this winter."

I insert the foregoing as being of much interest, it having been frequently stated that the wild Cat will not mate with the domestic Cat. The kitten offered to me is now at Fawley Court, Bucks.

Among the numerous letters I have received from America is one from Mrs. Mary A. C. Livermore, of Cambridge, Mass., U.S.A., who writes: "I have just come possessed of a black long-haired Cat from Maine. It is neither Persian, Angora, nor Indian. They are called here 'Coon' Cats, and it is vulgarly supposed to be a cross between a common Cat and a 'Coon.' Mine is a rusty bear-brown colour, but his relatives have been black and white, blue and white, and fawn and white, the latter the gentlest, prettiest Cat I know. His tail is very bushy and a fine ruff adorns his neck. A friend of mine has a pair of these Cats, all black, and the female consorts with no one but her mate. Yet often she has in her litter a common short-haired kitten."

Since the above reached me, I have received from another correspondent in the United States a very beautiful photograph of what is termed a "Coon" Cat. It certainly differs much from the ordinary long-haired Cat in appearance; but as to its being a cross with the Racoon, such a supposition is totally out of the question, and the idea cannot be entertained. The photographs sent to me show that the ears are unusually large, the head long, the length being in excess from the eyes to the tip of the nose, the legs and feet are large and evenly covered with long, somewhat coarse hair, the latter being devoid of tufts between and at the extremity of the toes; there are no long hairs of any consequence either within the ears or at their apex. The frill or mane is considerable, as is the length of the hair covering the body; the tail is rather short and somewhat thick, well covered with hair of equal length, and in shape like a fox's brush. The eyes are large, round, and full, with a wild staring expression. Certainly, the breed, however it may be obtained, is most interesting to the Cat naturalist, and the colour, as before stated, being peculiar, must of course attract his attention independently of its general appearance.

Since the above was written, I have received the following from Mr. Henry Brooker, The Elms, West Midford, Massachusetts, United States of America. After asking for information respecting Cats of certain breeds, he says: "I have had for a number of years a peculiar strain of long-haired Cats; they come from the islands off the coast of Maine, and are known in this country as 'Coon' Cats. The belief is that they have been crossed with the 'Coon.' This, of course, is untrue. The inhabitants of these islands are seafaring people, and many years ago some one on his vessel had a pair of long-haired Cats from which the strain has sprung. There are few short-haired cats on the island as there is no communication with the mainland except by boat. I want to improve my strain and get finer hair than the Cats now have. Yellow Cats are the most popular kind here, and I have succeeded in producing Cats of a rich mahogany colour with brushes like a fox. They hunt in the fields with me, and my Scotch terriers and they are on the most friendly terms." This, as a corroboration of the foregoing letters and the photographs, is, I take it, eminently satisfactory.

I have been shown a Siberian Cat, by Mr. Castang, of Leadenhall Market; the breed is entirely new to me. It is a small female Cat of a slaty-blue colour, rather short in body and legs; the head is small and much rounded, while the ears are of medium size.

The iris of the eyes is a deep golden colour, which, in contrast to the bluish colour of the fur, makes them to appear still more brilliant; the tail is short and thick, very much so at the base, and suddenly pointed at the tip. It is particularly timid and wild in its nature, and is difficult to approach; but, as Mr. Castang observed, this timidity may be "because it does not understand our language and does not know when it is called or spoken to." I think it would make a valuable Cat to cross with some English varieties.

A correspondent writes: "In your book on Cats you do not mention Norwegian Cats. I was in Norway last year, and was struck by the Cats being different to any I had ever seen, being much stouter built, with thick close fur, mostly sandy, with stripes of dark yellow." I suppose I am to infer that both the sexes are of sandy yellow colour. If so, I should say it is more a matter of selection than a new colour. I find generally in the colder countries the fur is short, dense, and somewhat woolly, and as a rule, judging from the information that I am continually receiving, whole or entire colours predominate.

Large Cats are by some sought after. This, I take it, is a great mistake, the fairly medium-sized Cat being much the handsomer of the two, and they are generally also devoid of that coarseness that is found apparent in the former; while small Cats are extremely pretty, and I understand are not only likely to be "in vogue," but are actually now being bred for their extreme *prettiness*. I have heard of some of these "Bantam" Cats being produced by that true and most excellent fancier, Mr. Herbert Young, who not only has produced a Tortoiseshell Tom Cat on lines laid down by myself, but is also engaged in breeding more, and I have not the least doubt he will be most successful, he having so been in producing new colours and some of the finest silver tabby short-haired Cats as yet seen; these short-haired Cats, in my opinion, far surpassing for beauty any long-hair ever exhibited, and are certainly of a "sweeter disposition."

In my former edition of "Our Cats," I wrote hopefully and

expectantly of much good to be derived from the institution of the so-called National Cat Club, and of which I was then President; but I am sorry to say that none of those hopes or expectations have been realised, and I now feel the *deepest regret* that I was ever induced to be in any way associated with it. I do not care to go into particulars further than to say I found the principal idea of many of its members consisted not so much in promoting the welfare of the Cat as of winning prizes, and more particularly their own Cat Club medals, for which, though offered at public shows, the public were not allowed to compete, and when won by the members, in many cases the public were thoughtlessly misled by believing it was an open competition. I therefore felt it my duty to leave the club for that and other reasons. I have also left off judging of the Cats, even at my old much-loved show at the Crystal Palace, because I no longer cared to come into contact with *such* "Lovers of Cats."

I am very much in favour of the Cats' Homes. The one at Dublin, in which Miss Swift takes so much interest; the one in London, with Miss Mayhew working for it with the zeal of a true "Cat lover"; and that where Mr. Colam is the manager, all deserve and *have* my *sincerest* and *warmest* approbation, sympathy, and support, standing out as they do in such bright contrast to those self-styled "Cat lovers," the National Cat Club.

HARRISON WEIR, F.R.H.S.
"Iddesleigh," Sevenoaks,
March 12th, 1892.

With all good wishes,
Yours Truly
Harrison Weir
1889

A reduction of the large black Cat's Head.

*Drawn for the Posting Bill giving notice
of the first Cat Show at the Crystal Palace,
July 16, 1871.*

OUR CATS
AND
ALL ABOUT THEM

INTRODUCTORY

After a Cat Show at the Crystal Palace, I usually receive a number of letters requesting information. One asks: "What is a true tortoiseshell like?" Another: "What is a tabby?" and yet another: "What is a blue tabby?" One writes of the "splendid disposition" of his cat, another asks how to cure a cat scratching the furniture, and so on.

After much consideration, and also at the request of many, I have thought it best to publish my notes on cats, their ways, habits, instincts, peculiarities, usefulness, colours, markings, forms, and other qualities that are required as fitting subjects to exhibit at what is now one of the instituted exhibitions of "The land we live in," and also the Folk and other lore, both ancient and modern, respecting them.

It is many years ago that, when thinking of the large number of cats kept in London alone, I conceived the idea that it would be well to hold "Cat Shows," so that the different breeds, colours, markings, etc., might be more carefully attended to, and the domestic cat, sitting in front of the fire, would then possess a beauty and an attractiveness to its owner unobserved and unknown because uncultivated heretofore. Prepossessed with this view of the subject, I called on my friend Mr. Wilkinson, the then manager of the Crystal Palace. With his usual businesslike clear-headedness, he saw it was "a thing to be done." In a few days I presented my scheme in full working order: the schedule of prizes, the price of entry, the number of classes, and the points by which they would be judged, the number of prizes in each class, their amount, the different varieties of colour, form, size, and sex for which they were to be given; I also made a drawing of the head of a cat to be printed in black on yellow paper for a posting bill. Mr. F. Wilson, the Company's naturalist and show manager, then took the matter in charge, worked hard, got a goodly number of cats together, among which was my blue tabby, "The Old Lady," then about fourteen years old, yet the best in the show of its colour and never surpassed, though lately possibly equalled. To my watch-chain I have attached the silver bell she wore at her *début*.

My brother, John Jenner Weir, the Rev. J. Macdona, and myself acted as judges, and the result was a success far beyond our most sanguine expectations—so much so that I having made it a labour of love of the feline race, and acting "without fee, gratuity, or reward," the Crystal Palace Company generously presented me with a large silver tankard in token of their high approval of my exertions on behalf of "the Company," and—Cats. Now that a Cat Club is formed, shows are more numerous, and the entries increasing, there is every reason to expect a permanent benefit in every way to one of the most intelligent of (though often much abused) animals.

THE FIRST CAT SHOW

On the day for judging, at Ludgate Hill I took a ticket and the train for the Crystal Palace. Sitting alone in the comfortable cushioned compartment of a "first class," I confess I felt somewhat more than anxious as to the issue of the experiment. Yes; what would it be like? Would there be many cats? How many? How would the animals comport themselves in their cages? Would they sulk or cry for liberty, refuse all food? or settle down and take the situation quietly and resignedly, or give way to terror? I could in no way picture to myself the scene; it was all so new. Presently, and while I was musing on the subject, the door was opened, and a friend got in. "Ah!" said he, "how are you?" "Tolerably well," said I; "I am on my way to the Cat Show." "What!" said my friend, "that surpasses everything! A show of cats! Why, I hate the things; I drive them off my premises when I see them. You'll have a fine bother with them in their cages! Or are they to be tied up? Anyhow, what a noise there will be, and how they will clutch at the bars and try and get out, or they will strangle themselves with their chains." "I am sorry, very sorry," said I, "that you do not like cats. For my part, I think them extremely beautiful, also very graceful in all their actions, and they are quite as domestic in their habits as the dog, if not more so. They are very useful in catching rats and mice; they are not deficient in sense; they will jump up at doors to push up latches with their paws. I have known them knock at a door by the knocker when wanting admittance. They know Sunday from the week-day, and do not go out to wait for the meat barrow on that day; they—" "Stop," said my friend, "I see you do like cats, and I do not, so let the matter drop." "No," said I, "not so. That is why I instituted this Cat Show; I wish every one to see how beautiful a well-cared-for cat is, and how docile,

30

gentle, and—may I use the term?—cossetty. Why should not the cat that sits purring in front of us before the fire be an object of interest, and be selected for its colour, markings, and form? Now come with me, my dear old friend, and see the first Cat Show."

Inside the Crystal Palace stood my friend and I. Instead of the noise and struggles to escape, there lay the cats in their different pens, reclining on crimson cushions, making no sound save now and then a homely purring, as from time to time they lapped the nice new milk provided for them. Yes, there they were, big cats, very big cats, middling-sized cats, and small cats, cats of all colours and markings, and beautiful pure white Persian cats; and as we passed down the front of the cages I saw that my friend became interested; presently he said: "What a beauty this is! and here's another!" "And no doubt," said I, "many of the cats you have seen before would be quite as beautiful if they were as well cared for, or at least cared for at all; generally they are driven about and ill-fed, and often ill-used, simply for the reason that they are cats, and for no other. Yet I feel a great pleasure in telling you the show would have been much larger were it not for the difficulty of inducing the owners to send their pets from home, though you see the great care that is taken of them." "Well, I had no idea there was such a variety of form, size, and colour," said my friend, and departed. A few months after, I called on him; he was at luncheon, with two cats on a chair beside him—pets I should say, from their appearance.

This is not a solitary instance of the good of the first Cat Show in leading up to the observation of, and kindly feeling for, the domestic cat. Since then, throughout the length and breadth of the land there have been Cat Shows, and much interest is taken in them by all classes of the community, so much so that large prices have been paid for handsome specimens. It is to be hoped that by these shows the too often despised cat will meet with the attention and kind treatment that every dumb animal should have and ought to receive at the hands of humanity. Even the few instances of the shows generating a love for cats that have come before my own notice are a sufficient pleasure to me not to regret having thought out and planned the first Cat Show at the Crystal Palace.

HABITS

Before attempting to describe the different varieties, I should like to make a few remarks as to the habits and ways of "the domestic cat."

When judging, I have frequently found some of the exhibits of anything but a mild and placid disposition. Some have displayed a downright ferocity; others, on the contrary, have been excessively gentle, and very few but seemed to recognise their position, and submitted quietly to their confinement. This is easily accounted for when persons are accustomed to cats; they know what wonderful powers of observation the cat possesses, and how quickly they recognise the "why and the wherefore" of many things. Take for instance, how very *many* cats will open a *latched* door by springing up and holding on with one fore-leg while with the other they press down the latch catch, and so open the door; and yet even more observant are they than that, as I have shown by a case in my "Animal Stories, Old and New," in which a cat opened a door by pulling it *towards* him, when he found *pushing* it of no avail. The cat is more critical in noticing than the dog. I never knew but one dog that would open a door by moving the fastening without being shown or taught how to do it. Cats that have done so are numberless. I noticed one at the last Crystal Palace Show, a white cat: it looked up, it looked down, then to the right and then a little to the left, paused, seemed lost in thought, when, not seeing any one about, it crept up to the door, and with its paw tried to pull back the bolt or catch. On getting sight of me, it retired to a corner of the cage, shut its eyes, and pretended to sleep. I stood further away, and soon saw the paw coming through the bars again. This cat had noticed how the cage-door was fastened, and so knew how to open it.

Many cats that are said to be spiteful are made so by ill-treatment, for, as a rule, I have found them to be most affectionate and gentle, and that to the last degree, attaching themselves to individuals, although such is stated not to be the case, yet of this I am certain. Having had several in my house at one time, I found that no two were the "followers" of the same member of my family. But it may be argued, and I think with some degree of justice, Why was this? Was it only that each cat had a separate liking? If so, why? Why should not three or four cats take a liking to the same individual? But they seldom or never do, and for that matter there seems somewhat the same feeling with dogs. This required some consideration, but that not of long duration. For I am sorry to say I rapidly came to the conclusion that it was jealousy. Yes, jealousy! There was no doubt of it. Zeno would be very cossetty, loving, lovable, and gentle, but when Lulu came in and was nursed he retired to a corner and seized the first opportunity of vanishing through the door. As soon as Zillah jumped on my knee and put her paws about my neck, Lulu looked at me, then at her, then at me, walked to the fire, sat down, looked round, got up, went to the door, cried to go out, the door was opened, and—she fled. I thought that Zillah seemed then more than ever—happy.

Though jealousy is one of if not the ruling attributes of the cat, there are exceptions to such a rule. Sometimes it may be that two or more will take to the same person. As an instance of this I had two cats, one a red tabby, a great beauty; Lillah, a short-haired red-and-white cat; the latter and a white long-haired one, named "The Colonel," were great friends, and these associated with a tortoiseshell-and-white, Lizzie. None of these were absolutely house cats, but attended more to the poultry yards and runs, looking after the chicken, seeing that no rats were about or other "vermin," near the coops. Useful cats, very!

Mine was then a very large garden, and generally of an evening, when at home, I used to walk about the numerous paths to admire the beauties of the different herbaceous plants, of which I had an interesting collection. Five was my time of starting on my ambulation, when, on going out of the door, I was sure to find the two first-named cats, and often the third, waiting for me, ready to go wherever I went, following like faithful dogs. These apparently never had any jealous feeling.

Of all the cats Lillah was the most loving. If I stood still, she would look up, and watch the expression of my face. If she thought it was favourable to her, she would jump, and, clinging to my chest, put her fore-paws around my neck, and rub her head softly against my face, purring melodiously all the time, then move on to my shoulder, while "The Colonel" and his tortoiseshell friend Lizzie would press about my legs, uttering the same musical self-complacent sound. Here, there, and everywhere, even out into the road or into the wood, the pretty things would accompany me, seeming intensely happy. When I returned to the house, they would scamper off, bounding in the air, and playing with and tumbling over each other in the fullest and most frolicsome manner imaginable. No! I do not think that Lillah, The Colonel, or Lizzie ever knew the feeling of jealousy. But these, as I said before, were exceptions. They all had a sad ending, coming to an untimely death through being caught in wires set by poachers for rabbits. I have ever regretted the loss of the gentle Lillah. She was as beautiful as she was good, gentle, and loving, without a fault.

It may have been noted in the foregoing I have said that my cats were always awaiting my coming. Just so. The cat seems to take note of time as well as place. At my town house I had a cat named Guadalquiver, which was fed on horseflesh brought to the door. Every day during the week he would go and sit ready for the coming of "the cat's-meat man," but he never did so on the Sunday. How it was he knew on that day that the man did not come I never could discover; still, the fact remains. How he, or whether he, counted the days until the sixth, and then rested the seventh from his watching, is a mystery. A similar case is related of an animal belonging to Mr. Trübncr, the London publisher.

The cat, a gigantic one, and a pet of his, used to go every evening to the end of the terrace, on which was the house where he resided, to escort Mr. Trübner back to dinner on his arrival from the City, but was never once known to make the mistake of going to meet him on Sundays. And again, how well a cat knows when it is luncheon-time! He or she may be apparently asleep on the tiles, or snugly lying under a bush basking in the sun's warm rays, when it will look up, yawn, stretch itself, get up, and move leisurely towards the house, and as the luncheon-bell rings, in walks the cat, as ready for food as any there.

Most cats are of a gentle disposition, but resent ill-treatment in a most determined way, generally making use of their claws, at the same time giving vent to their feelings by a low growl and spitting furiously. Under such conditions it is best to leave off that which has appeared to irritate them. Dogs generally bite when they lose their temper, but a cat seldom. Should a cat dig her claws into your hand, never draw it backward, but push forward; you thus close the foot and render the claws harmless. If otherwise, you generally lose three to four pieces of skin from your hand; the cat knows he has done it, and feels revenged. Some cats do not like their ears touched, others their backs, others their tails. I have one now (Fritz); he has such a great dislike to having his tail touched that if we only point to it and say "Tail!" he growls, and if repeated he will get up and go out of the room, even though he was enjoying the comfort of his basket before a good fire. By avoiding anything that is known to tease an animal, no matter what, it will be found that is the true way, combined with gentle treatment and oft caressing, to tame and to make them love you, even those whose temper is none of the best. This is equally applicable to horses, cows, and dogs as to cats. Gentleness and kindness will work wonders with animals, and, I take it, is not lost on human beings.

The distance cats will travel to find and regain the home they have been taken from is surprising. One my groom begged of me, as he said he had no cat at home, and he was fond of "the dear thing," but he really wanted to be rid of it, as I found afterwards. He took the poor animal away in a hamper, and after carrying it some three miles through London streets, threw it into the Surrey Canal. That cat was sitting wet and dirty outside the stable when he came in the morning, and went in joyfully on his opening the door, ran up to and climbed on to the back of its favourite, the horse, who neighed a "welcome home." The man left that week.

Another instance, and I could give many more, but this will suffice. It is said that if you wish an old cat to stay you should have the mother with the kitten or kittens, but this sometimes fails to keep her. Having a fancy for a beautiful brown tabby, I purchased her and kitten from a cottager living two miles and a half away. The next day I let her out, keeping the kitten in a basket before the fire. In half an hour mother and child were gone, and though she had to carry her little one through woods, hedgerows, across grass and arable fields, she arrived home with her young charge quite safely the following day, though evidently very tired, wet, and hungry. After two days she was brought back, and being well fed and carefully tended, she roamed no more.

The cat, like many other animals, will often form singular attachments. One would sit in my horse's manger and purr and rub against his nose, which undoubtedly the horse enjoyed, for he would frequently turn his head purposely to be so treated. One went as consort with a Dorking cock; another took a great liking to my collie, Rover; another loved Lina, the cow; while another would cosset up close to a sitting hen, and allowed the fresh-hatched chickens to seek warmth by creeping under her. Again, they will rear other animals such as rats, rabbits, squirrels, puppies, hedgehogs; and, when motherly inclined, will take to almost anything, even to a young pigeon.

At the Brighton Show of 1886 there were two cats, both reared by dogs, the foster-mother and her bantling showing evident signs of sincere affection.

There are both men and women who have a decided antipathy to cats—"Won't have one in the house on any account." They are called "deceitful," and some go as far as to say "treacherous," but how and in what way I cannot discover. Others, on the contrary, love cats beyond all other "things domestic." Of course cats, like other animals, or even human beings, are very dissimilar, no two being precisely alike in disposition, any more than are to be found two forms so closely resembling as not to be distinguished one from the other. To some a cat is a cat, and if all were black all would be alike. But this would not be so in reality, as those well know who are close observers of animal and bird life. Of course the gamekeeper has a dislike to cats, more especially when they "take to the woods," but so long as they are fed, and keep within bounds, they are "useful" in scaring away rats from the young broods of pheasants. What are termed "poaching cats" are clearly "outlaws," and must be treated as such.

TRAINED CATS

That cats may be trained to respect the lives of other animals, and also birds on which they habitually feed, is a well-known fact. In proof of this I well recollect a story that my father used to tell of "a happy family" that was shown many years ago on the Surrey side of Waterloo Bridge. Their abode consisted of a large wire cage placed on wheels. In windy weather the "breezy side" was protected by green baize, so draughts were prevented, and a degree of comfort obtained. As there was no charge for "the show," a box was placed in front with an opening for the purpose of admitting any donations from those who felt inclined to give. On it was written "The Happy Family—their money-box." The family varied somewhat, as casualties occurred occasionally by death from natural causes or sales. Usually, there was a Monkey, an Owl, some Guinea-pigs, Squirrels, small birds, Starlings, a Magpie, Rats, Mice, and a Cat or two. But the story? Well, the story is this. One day, when my father was looking at "the happy family," a burly-looking man came up, and, after a while, said to the man who owned the show: "Ah! I don't see much in that. It is true the cat does not touch the small birds [one of which was sitting on the head of the cat at the time], nor the other things; but you could not manage to keep rats and mice in there as well." "Think not?" said the showman. "I think I could very easily." "Not you," said the burly one. "I will give you a month to do it in, if you like, and a shilling in the bargain if you succeed. I shall be this way again soon." "Thank you, sir," said the man. "Don't go yet," then, putting a stick through the bars of the cage he lifted up the cat, when from beneath her out ran a white rat and three white mice. "Won—der—ful!" slowly ejaculated he of the burly form; "Wonder—ful!" The money was paid.

Cats, properly trained, will not touch anything, alive or dead, on the premises to which they are attached. I have known them to sport with tame rabbits, to romp and jump in frolicsome mood this way, then that, which both seemed greatly to enjoy, yet they would bring home wild rabbits they had killed, and not touch my little chickens or ducklings.

"The Old Lady"

When I built a house in the country, fond as I am of cats, I determined *not* to keep any there, because they would destroy the birds' nests and drive my feathered friends away, and I liked to watch and feed these from the windows. Things went pleasantly for awhile. The birds were fed, and paid for their keep with many and many a song. There were the old ones and there the young, and oft by the hour I watched them from the window; and they became so tame as scarcely caring to get out of my way when I went outside with more food. But—there is always a but— but one day, or rather evening, as I was "looking on," a rat came out from the rocks, and then another. Soon they began their repast on the remains of the birds' food. Then in the twilight

40

came mice, the short-tailed and the long, scampering hither and thither. This, too, was amusing. In the autumn I bought some filberts, and put them into a closet upstairs, went to London, returned, and thought I would sleep in the room adjoining the closet. No such thing. As soon as the light was out there was a sound of gnawing—curb—curb—sweek!—squeak—a rushing of tiny feet here, there, and everywhere; thump, bump—scriggle, scraggle—squeak—overhead, above the ceiling, behind the skirting boards, under the floor, and—in the closet. I lighted a candle, opened the door, and looked into the repository for my filberts. What a hustling, what a scuffling, what a scrambling. There they were, mice in numbers; they "made for" some holes in the corners of the cupboard, got jammed, squeaked, struggled, squabbled, pushed, their tails making circles; push—push—squeak!—more jostling, another effort or two—squeak—squeak—gurgle—squeak—more struggling—and they were gone. Gone? Yes! but not for long. As soon as the light was out back they came. No! oh, dear no! sleep! no more sleep. Outside, I liked to watch the mice; but when they climbed the ivy and got inside, the pleasure entirely ceased. Nor was this all; they got into the vineries and spoilt the grapes, and the rats killed the young ducks and chickens, and undermined the building also, besides storing quantities of grain and other things under the floor. The result number one was, three cats coming on a visit. Farmyard cats—cats that knew the difference between chickens, ducklings, mice, and rats. Result number two, that after being away a couple of weeks, I went again to my cottage, and I slept undisturbed in the room late the play-ground of the mice. My chickens and ducklings were safe, and soon the cats allowed the birds to be fed in front of the window, though I could not break them of destroying many of the nests. I never noticed more fully the very great use the domestic cat is to man than on that occasion. All day my cats were indoors, dozy, sociable, and contented. At night they were on guard outside, and doubtless saved me the lives of dozens of my "young things." One afternoon I saw one of my cats coming towards me with apparent difficulty in walking. On its near approach I found it was carrying a large rat, which appeared dead. Coming nearer, the cat put down the rat. Presently I saw it move, then it suddenly got up and ran off. The cat caught it again. Again it feigned death, again got up and ran off, and was once more caught. It laid quite still, when, perceiving the cat had turned away, it got up, apparently quite uninjured, and ran in another direction, and I and the cat—lost it! I was not sorry. This rat deserved his liberty. Whether it was permanent I know not, as "Little-john," the cat, remained, and I left.

The cat is not only a very useful animal about the house and premises, but is also ornamental. It is lithe and beautiful in form, and graceful in action. Of course there are cats that are ugly by comparison with others, both in form, colour, and markings; and as there are now cat shows, at which prizes are offered for varieties, I will endeavour to give, in succeeding chapters, the points of excellence as regards form, colour, and markings required and most esteemed for the different classes. I am the more induced to define these as clearly as possible, owing to the number of mistakes that often occur in the entries.

LONG-HAIRED CATS

These are very diversified, both in form, colour, and the quality of the hair, which in some is more woolly than in others; and they vary also in the shape and length of the tail, the ears, and size of eyes. There are several varieties—the Russian, the Angora, the Persian, and Indian. Forty or fifty years ago they used all to be called French cats, as they were mostly imported from Paris—more particularly the white, which were then the fashion, and, if I remember rightly, they, as a rule, were larger than those of the present day. Coloured long-haired cats were then rare, and but little cared for or appreciated. The pure white, with long silky hair, bedecked with blue or rose-colour ribbon, or a silver collar with its name inscribed thereon or one of scarlet leather studded with brass, might often be seen stretching its full lazy length on luxurious woollen rugs—the valued, pampered pets of "West End" life.

A curious fact relating to the white cat of not only the long but also the short-haired breed is their deafness. Should they have blue eyes, which is the fancy colour, these are nearly always deaf; although I have seen specimens whose hearing was as perfect as that of any other colour. Still deafness in white cats is not always confined to those with blue eyes, as I too well know from purchasing a very fine male at the Crystal Palace Show some few years since. The price was low and the cat "a beauty," both in form, coat, and tail, his eyes were yellow, and he had a nice, meek, mild, expressive face. I stopped and looked at him, as he much took my fancy. He stared at me wistfully, with something like melancholy in the gaze of his *amber*-coloured eyes. I put my hand through the bars of the cage. He purred, licked my hand, rubbed against the wires, put his tail up, as much as to say, "See,

43

here is a beautiful tail; am I not a lovely cat?" "Yes," thought I, "a very nice cat."

When I looked at my catalogue and saw the low price, "something is wrong here," said I, musingly. "Yes, there *must* be something wrong. The price is misstated, or there is something not right about this cat." No! it was a beauty—so comely, so loving, so gentle—so very gentle. "Well," said I to myself, "if there is no misstatement of price, I will buy this cat," and, with a parting survey of its excellences, I went to the office of the show manager. He looked at the letter of entry. No; the price was quite right—"two guineas!" "I will buy it," said I. And so I did; but at two guineas I bought it dearly. Yes! very dearly, for when I got it home I found it was "stone" deaf. What an unhappy cat it was! If shut out of the dining-room you could hear its cry for admission all over the house; being so deaf the poor wretched creature never knew the noise it made. I often wish that it had so known—very, very often. I am satisfied that a tithe would have frightened it out of its life. And so loving, so affectionate. But, oh! horror, when it called out as it sat on my lap, its voice seemed to acquire at least *ten cat power*. And when, if it lost sight of me in the garden, its voice rose to the occasion, I feel confident it might have been heard miles off. Alas! he never knew what that agonised sound was like, but I did, and I have never forgotten it, and I never shall. I named him "The Colonel" on account of his commanding voice.

One morning a friend came—blessed be that day—and after dinner he saw "the beauty." "What a lovely cat!" said he. "Yes," said I, "he is very beautiful, quite a picture." After a while he said, looking at "Pussy" warming himself before the fire, "I think I never saw one I liked more." "Indeed," said I, "if you really think so, I will give it to you; but he has a fault—he is 'stone' deaf." "Oh, I don't mind that," said he. He took him away—miles and miles away. I was glad it was so many miles away for two reasons. One was I feared he might come back, and the other that his voice might come resounding on the still night air. But he never came back nor a sound.—A few days after he left "to better himself," a letter came saying, would I wish to have him back? They liked it very much, all but its voice. "No," I wrote, "no, you are very kind, no, thank you; give him to any one you please—do what you will with 'the beauty,' but it must not return, never." When next I saw my friend, I asked him how "the beauty" was. "You dreadful man!" said he; "why, that cat nearly drove us all mad—I never heard anything like it." "Nor I," said I, sententiously. "Well," said my friend, "'all is well that ends well,' I have given it to a very deaf old lady, and so both are happy." "Very, I trust," said I.

The foregoing is by way of advice; in buying a white cat—or, in fact, any other—ascertain for a *certainty* that it is *not deaf.*

A short time since I saw a white Persian cat with deep blue eyes sitting at the door of a tobacconist's, at the corner of the Haymarket, London. On inquiry I found that the cat could hear perfectly, and was in no way deficient of health and strength; and this is by no means a solitary instance.

Miss Saunders' "Tiger."

THE ANGORA

The Angora cat, as its name indicates, comes from Angora, in Western Asia, a province that is also celebrated for its goats with long hair, which is of extremely fine quality. It is said that this deteriorates when the animal leaves that locality. This may be so, but that I have no means of proving; yet, if so, do the Angora cats also deteriorate in the silky qualities of their fur? Or does it get shorter? Certain it is that many of the imported cats have finer and longer hair than those bred in this country; but when are the latter true bred? Even some a little cross-bred will often have long hair, but not of the texture as regards length and silkiness which is to be noted in the pure breed.

The Angora cats, I am told, are great favourites with the Turks and Armenians, and the best are of high value, a pure white, with blue eyes, being thought the perfection of cats, all other points being good, and its hearing by no means defective. The points are a small head, with not too long a nose, large full eyes of a colour in harmony with that of its fur, ears rather large than small and pointed, with a tuft of hair at the apex, the size not showing, as they are deeply set in the long hair on the forehead, with a very full flowing mane about the head and neck; this latter should not be short, neither the body, which should be long, graceful, and elegant, and covered with long, silky hair, with a slight admixture of woolliness; in this it differs from the Persian, and the longer the better.

In texture it should be as fine as possible, and also not so woolly as that of the Russian; still it is more inclined to be so than the Persian. The legs to be of moderate length, and in proportion to the body; the tail long, and slightly curving upward towards the end. The hair should be very long at the base, less so toward the tip. When perfect, it is an extremely beautiful and elegant object, and no wonder that it has become a pet among the Orientals. The colours are varied; but the black which should have orange eyes, as should also the slate colours, and blues, and the white are the most esteemed, though the soft slates, blues, and the light fawns, deep reds, and mottled grays are shades of colour that blend well with the Eastern furniture and other surroundings.

There are also light grays, and what is termed smoke colour; a beauty was shown at Brighton which was white with black tips to the hair, the white being scarcely visible, unless the hair was parted; this tinting had a marvellous effect. I have never seen imported strong-coloured tabbies of this breed, nor do I believe such are true Angoras. Fine specimens are even now rare in this country, and are extremely valuable. In manners and temper they are quiet, sociable, and docile, though given to roaming, especially in the country, where I have seen them far from their homes, hunting the hedgerows more like dogs than cats; nor do they appear to possess the keen intelligence of the short-haired European cat.

They are not new to us, being mentioned by writers nearly a hundred years ago, if not more. I well remember white specimens of uncommon size on sale in Leadenhall Market, more than forty years since; the price usually was five guineas, though some of rare excellence would realise double that sum.

Miss Moore's "Dinah."

Miss Saunders' "Sylvie."

THE PERSIAN CAT

This differs somewhat from the Angora, the tail being generally longer, more like a table brush in point of form, and is generally slightly turned upwards, the hair being more full and coarser at the end, while at the base it is somewhat longer. The head is rather larger, with less pointed ears, although these should not be devoid of the tuft at the apex, and also well furnished with long hair within, and of moderate size. The eyes should be large, full, and round, with a soft expression; the hair on the forehead is generally rather short in comparison to the other parts of the body, which ought to be clothed with long silky hair, very long about the neck, giving the appearance of the mane of the lion. The legs, feet, and toes should be well clothed with long hair and have well-developed fringes on the toes, assuming the character of tufts between them. It is larger in body, and generally broader in the loins, and apparently stronger made, than the foregoing variety, though yet slender and elegant, with small bone, and exceedingly graceful in all its movements, there being a kind of languor observable in its walk, until roused, when it immediately assumes the quick motion of the ordinary short-haired cat, though not so alert. The colours vary very much, and comprise almost every tint obtainable in cats, though the tortoiseshell is not, nor is the dark marked tabby, in my opinion, a Persian cat colour, but has been got by crossing with the short-haired tortoiseshell, and also English tabby, and as generally shows pretty clearly unmistakable signs of such being the case. For a long time, if not now, the black was the most sought after and the most difficult to obtain. A good rich, deep black, with orange-coloured eyes and long flowing hair, grand in mane, large and with graceful carriage, with a mild expression, is truly a very beautiful object, and one very rare. The best I have hitherto seen was one that belonged to Mr. Edward Lloyd, the great authority on all matters relating to aquariums. It was called Mimie, and was a very fine specimen, usually carrying off the first prize wherever shown. It generally wore a handsome collar, on which was inscribed its name and victories. The collar, as Mr. Lloyd used jocosely to observe, really belonged to it, as it was bought out of its winnings; and, according to the accounts kept, was proved also to have paid for its food for some considerable period. It was, as its owner laughingly said, "his friend, and not his dependent," and generally used to sit on the table by his side while he was writing either his letters, articles, or planning those improvements regarding aquariums, for which he was so justly celebrated.

Next in value is the light slate or blue colour. This beautiful tint is very different in its shades. In some it verges towards a light purplish or lilac hue, and is very lovely; in others it tends to a much bluer tone, having a colder and harder appearance, still beautiful by way of contrast; in all the colour should be pure, even, and bright, not in any way mottled, which is a defect; and I may here remark that in these colours the hair is generally of a softer texture, as far as I have observed, than that of any other colour, not excepting the white, which is also in much request. Then follow the various shades of light tabbies, so light in the marking having scarcely a right to be called tabbies; in fact, tabby is not a Persian colour, nor have I ever seen an imported cat of that colour—I mean firmly, strongly marked with black on a brown-blue or gray ground, until they culminate in those of intense richness and density in the way of deep, harmonious browns and reds, yet still preserving throughout an extreme delicacy of line and tracery, never becoming harsh or hard in any of its arrangements or colour; not as the ordinary short-haired tabby. The eyes should be orange-yellow in the browns, reds, blues, grays, and blacks.

As far as my experience extends, and I have had numerous opportunities of noticing, I find this variety less reliable as regards temper than the short-haired cats, less also in the keen sense of observing, as in the Angora, and also of turning such observations to account, either as regards their comfort, their endeavour to help themselves, or in their efforts to escape from confinement.

In some few cases I have found them to be of almost a savage disposition, biting and snapping more like a dog than a cat, and using their claws less for protective purposes. Nor have I found them so "cossetty" in their ways as those of the "short-coats," though I have known exceptions in both.

Mr. A. A. Clarke's "Tim."

They are much given to roam, as indeed are the Russian and Angora, especially in the country, going considerable distances either for their own pleasure or in search of food, or when "on the hunt." After mature consideration, I have come to the conclusion that this breed, and slightly so the preceding, are decidedly different in their habits to the short-haired English domestic cat, as it is now generally called.

It may be, however, only a very close observer would notice the several peculiarities which I consider certainly exist. These cats attach themselves to places more than persons, and are indifferent to those who feed and have the care of them. They are beautiful and useful objects about the house, and generally very pleasant companions, and when kept with the short-haired varieties form an exceedingly pretty and interesting contrast; but, as I have stated, they certainly require more attention to their training, and more caution in their handling, than the latter. I may here remark, that during the time I have acted as judge at cat shows, which is now over eighteen years, it has been seldom there has been any display of temper in the short-haired breeds in comparison with the long; though some of the former, in some instances, have not comported themselves with that sweetness and amiability of disposition that is their usual characteristic. My attendant has been frequently wounded in our endeavour to examine the fur, dentition, etc., of the Angora, Persian, or Russian; and once severely by a "short-hair." Hitherto I have been so fortunate as to escape all injury, but this I attribute to my close observation of the *countenance* and expression of the cat about to be handled, so as to be perfectly on my guard, and to the knowledge of how to put my hands out of harm's way. If a vicious cat is to be taken from one pen to another, it must be carried by the loose skin at the back of the neck and that of the back with both hands, and held well away from the person who is carrying it.

THE RUSSIAN LONG-HAIRED CAT

The above is a portrait of a cat given me many years ago, whose parents came from Russia, but from what part I could never ascertain. It differed from the Angora and the Persian in many respects. It was larger in the body with shorter legs. The mane or frill was very large, long, and dense, and more of a woolly texture, with coarse hairs among it; the colour was of dark tabby, though the markings were not a decided black, nor clear and distinct; the ground colour was wanting in that depth and richness possessed by the Persian, having a somewhat dull appearance. The eyes were large and prominent, of a bright orange, slightly tinted with green, the ears large by comparison, with small tufts, full of long, woolly hair, the limbs stout and short, the tail being very dissimilar, as it was short, very woolly, and thickly covered with hair the same length from the base to the tip, and much resembled in form that of the English wild cat. Its motion was not so agile as other cats, nor did it apparently care for warmth, as it liked being outdoors in the coldest weather. Another peculiarity being that it seemed to care little in the way of watching birds for the purpose of food, neither were its habits like those of the short-haired cats that were its companions. It attached itself to no person, as was the case with some of the others, but curiously took a particular fancy to one of my short-haired, silver-gray tabbies; the two appeared always together. In front of the fire they sat side by side. If one left the room the other followed. Adown the garden paths there they were, still companions; and at night slept in the same box; they drank milk from the same saucer, and fed from the same plate, and, in fact, only seemed to exist for each other. In all my experience I never knew a more devoted couple. I bred but one kitten from the Russian, and this was the offspring of the short-haired silver tabby. It was black-and-white, and resembled the Russian in a large degree, having a woolly coat, somewhat of a mane, and a short, very bushy tail. This, like his father, seemed also to be fonder of animals for food than birds, and, although very small, would without any hesitation attack and kill a full-grown rat. I have seen several Russian cats, yet never but on this occasion had the opportunity of comparing their habits and mode of life with those of the other varieties; neither have I seen any but those of a tabby colour, and they mostly of a dark brown. I am fully aware that many cross-bred cats are sold as Russian, Angora, and Persian, either between these or the short-haired, and some of these, of course, retain in large degree the distinctive peculiarities of each breed. Yet to the practised eye there is generally—I do not say always—a difference of some sort by which the particular breed may be clearly defined. When the prizes are given, as is the case even at our largest cat shows, for the best long-haired cat, there, of course, exists in the eye of the judge no distinction as regards breed. He selects, as he is bound to do, that which is the best *long-haired* cat in all points, the length of hair, colour, texture, and condition of the exhibit being that which commands his first attention. But if it were so put that the prize should be for the best Angora, Persian, Russian, etc., it would make the task rather more than difficult, for I have seen some "first-cross cats" that have possessed all, or nearly all, the points requisite for that of the Angora, Persian, or Russian, while others so bred have been very deficient, perhaps showing the Angora cross only by the tail and a slight and small frill. At the same time it must be noted, that, although from time to time some excellent specimens may be so bred, it is by no means desirable to buy and use such for stock purposes, for they will in all probability "throw back"—that is, after several generations, although allied with thoroughbred, they will possibly have a little family of quite "short-hairs." I have known this with rabbits, who, after breeding short-haired varieties for some time, suddenly reverted to a litter of "long-hairs"; but have not carried out the experiment with cats. At the same time I may state that I have little or no doubt that such would be the case; therefore I would urge on all those who are fond of cats—or, in fact, other animals—of any particular breed, to use when possible none but those of the purest pedigree, as this will tend to prevent much disappointment that might otherwise ensue. But I am digressing, and so back to my subject—the Russian long-haired cat. I advisedly say long-haired cat, for I shall hereafter have to treat of other cats coming from Russia that are short-haired, none which I have hitherto seen being tabbies, but whole colour. This is the more singular as all those of the long-hair have been brown tabbies, with only one or two exceptions, which were black. It is just possible these were the offspring of tabby or gray parents, as the wild rabbit has been known to have had black progeny. I have seen a black rabbit shot from amongst the gray on the South Downs.

Miss Mary Gresham's Persian Kitten, "Lambkin."

I do not remember having seen a white Russian "long-hair," and I should feel particularly obliged to any of my readers who could supply me with further information on this subject, or on any other relating to the various breeds of cats, cat-life and habits. I am fully aware that no two cats are exactly alike either in their form, colour, movements, or habits; but what I have given much study and attention to, and what I wish to arrive at is, the broad existing natural distinctions of the different varieties. In this way I shall feel grateful for any information.

The above engraving and description of a very peculiar animal is from Daniel's "Rural Sports," 1813:

"This Cat was the Property of Mrs. Finch, of Maldon, Essex. In the Account of this *Lusus Naturæ*, for such it may be deemed, the *Mother* had no other Likeness to her Production, than her Colour, which is a *tawny Sandy*, in some parts lightly streaked with *black*; She had this, and another Kitten *like it*, about *two*

61

Years since. The fellow Kitten was killed, in consequence of being troublesome, to the Mistress of the House, where it was presented. *This* is a *Male*, above the *usual* Size, with a *shaggy* Appearance round its Face, resembling that of the Lion's, in *Miniature*. The *Hair* protruding from the *Ears*, formerly grew, like what are termed *Cork-screw Curls*, and which are frequently seen, among the *smart* young *Watermen*, on the Thames; the Tail is perfectly distinct, from that of the Cat Species, and resembles the *Brush* of a Fox. The Mother, has at this time (1813), three Young ones, but without the least Difference to *common* Kittens, neither, indeed, has she ever had any *before*, or since, similar to *That* here described. The Proprietor has been offered, and refused One Hundred Pounds for this Animal."

This was either a cross with the English wild cat, which sometimes has a mane, or it was an accidental variation of nature. I once bred a long-haired rabbit in a similar way, but at first I failed entirely to perpetuate the peculiarity. I think the above simply "a sport."

Miss Mary Gresham's Persian Kitten, "Lambkin No. 2."

Miss Moore's "Bogey."

I have now concluded my remarks on the long-haired varieties of cats that I am at present acquainted with. They are an exceedingly interesting section; their habits, manners, forms, and colours form a by no means unprofitable study for those fond of animal life, as they, in my opinion, differ in many ways from those of their "short-haired" brethren. I shall not cease, however, in my endeavours to find out if any other long-haired breeds exist, and I am, therefore, making inquiries in every direction in which I deem it likely I shall get an increase of information on the subject, but hitherto without any success. Therefore, I am led to suppose that the three I have enumerated are the only domesticated long-haired varieties. The nearest approach, I believe, to these in the wild state is that of the British wild cat, which has in some instances a mane and a bushy tail, slightly resembling that of the Russian long-hair, with much of the same facial expression, and rather pointed tufts at the apex of the ears. It is also large, like some of the "long-haired" cats that I have seen; in fact, it far more resembles these breeds than those of the short hair. I was much struck with the many points of similitude on seeing the British wild cat exhibited by the Duke of Sutherland at the first cat show at the Crystal Palace in July, 1871. I merely offer this as an idea for further consideration. At the same time, allow me to say that I have had no opportunity of studying the anatomy of the British wild cat, in contradistinction to that of the Russian, or others with long hair. I only wish to point out what I term a general resemblance, far in excess of those with short hair. I am fully aware how difficult it is to trace any origin of the domestic cat, or from what breeds; it is also said, that the British wild cat is not one of them, still I urge there exists the similarity I mention; whether it is so apparent to others I know not.

Mr. Smith's Prize He-Cat.

THE TORTOISESHELL CAT

I now come to the section of the short-haired domestic cat, a variety possessing sub-varieties. Whether these all came from the same origin is doubtful, although in breeding many of the different colours will breed back to the striped or tabby colour, and, *per contra*, white whole-coloured cats are often got from striped or spotted parents, and *vice versâ*. Those that have had any experience of breeding domesticated animals or birds, know perfectly well how difficult it is to keep certain peculiarities gained by years of perseverance of breeding for such points of variation, or what is termed excellence. Place a few fancy pigeons, for instance, in the country and let them match how they like, and one would be quite surprised, unless he were a naturalist, to note the great changes that occur in a few years, and the unmistakable signs of reversion towards their ancestral stock—that of the Rock pigeon. But with the cat this is somewhat different, as little or no attempts have been made, as far as I know of, until cat shows were instituted, to improve any particular breed either in form or colour. Nor has it even yet, with the exception of the long-haired cats. Why this is so I am at a loss to understand, but the fact remains. Good well-developed cats of certain colours fetch large prices, and are, if I may use the term, perpetual prize-winners. I will take as an instance the tortoiseshell tom, he, or male cat as one of the most scarce, and the red or yellow tabby she-cat as the next; and yet the possessor of either, with proper care and attention, I have little or no doubt, has it in his power to produce either variety *ad libitum*. It is now many years since I remember the first "tortoiseshell tom-cat;" nor can I now at this distance of time quite call to mind whether or not it was not a tortoiseshell-and-white, and not a tortoiseshell pure and simple. It was exhibited in Piccadilly. If I remember rightly, I made a drawing of it, but as it is about forty years ago, of this I am not certain, although I have lately been told that I did, and that the price asked for the cat was 100 guineas.

Example of Tortoiseshell cat, very dark variety.

This supposed scarcity was rudely put aside by the appearance, at the Crystal Palace Show of 1871, of no less than one tortoiseshell he-cat (exhibited by Mr. Smith) and three tortoiseshell-and-white he-cats, but it will be observed there was really but only one tortoiseshell he-cat, the others having white. On referring to the catalogues of the succeeding shows, no other pure tortoiseshell has been exhibited, and he ceased to appear after 1873; but tortoiseshell-and-white have been shown from 1871, varying in number from five to three until 1885. One of these, a tortoiseshell-and-white belonging to Mr. Hurry, gained no fewer than nine first prizes at the Crystal Palace, besides several firsts at other shows; this maintains my statement, that a really good scarce variety of cats is a valuable investment, Mr. Hurry's cat

Totty keeping up his price of £100 till the end.

As may have been gathered from the foregoing remarks, the points of the tortoiseshell he-cat are, black-red and yellow in patches, but no *white*. The colouring should be in broad, well-defined blotches and solid in colour, not mealy or tabby-like in the marking, but clear, sharp, and distinct, and the richer and deeper the colours the better. When this is so the animal presents a very handsome appearance. The eyes should be orange, the tail long and thick towards the base, the form slim, graceful, and elegant, and not too short on the leg, to which this breed has a tendency. Coming then to the actual tortoiseshell he, or male cat without white, I have never seen but one at the Shows, and that was exhibited by Mr. Smith. It does not appear that Mr. Smith bred any from it, nor do I know whether he took any precautions to do so; but if not, I am still of the opinion that more might have been produced. In Cassell's "Natural History," it is stated that the tortoiseshell cat is quite common in Egypt and in the south of Europe. This I can readily believe, as I think that it comes from a different stock than the usual short-haired cat, the texture of the hair being different, the form of tail also. I should much like to know whether in that country, where the variety is so common, there exists any number of tortoiseshell he-cats. In England the he-kittens are almost invariably red-tabby or red-tabby-and-white; the red-tabby she-cats are almost as scarce as tortoiseshell-and-white he-cats. Yet if red-tabby she-cats can be produced, I am of opinion that tortoiseshell he-cats could also. I had one of the former, a great beauty, and hoped to perpetuate the breed, but it unfortunately fell a victim to wires set by poachers for game. Again returning to the tortoiseshell, I have noted that, in drawings made by the Japanese, the cats are always of this colour; that being so, it leads one to suppose that in that country tortoiseshell he-cats must be plentiful. Though the drawings are strong evidence, they are not absolute proof. I have asked several travelling friends questions as regards the Japanese cats, but in no case have I found them to have taken sufficient notice for their testimony to be anything else than worthless. I shall be very thankful for any information on this subject, for to myself, and doubtless also to many others, it is exceedingly interesting. Any one wishing to breed rich brown tabbies, should use a tortoiseshell she-cat with a very brown and black-banded he-cat. They are not so good from the spotted tabby, often producing merely tortoiseshell tabbies instead of brown tabbies, or true tortoiseshells. My remarks as to the colouring of the tortoiseshell he-cat are equally applicable to the she-cat, which should not have any white. Of the tortoiseshell-and-white hereafter.

To breed tortoiseshell he-cats, I should use males of a whole colour, such as either white, black, or blue; and on no account any tabby, no matter the colour. What is wanted is patches of colour, not tiny streaks or spots; and I feel certain that, for those who persevere, there will be successful results.

THE TORTOISESHELL-AND-WHITE CAT

This is a more common mixture of colouring than the tortoiseshell pure and simple without white, and seems to be widely spread over different parts of the world. It is the opinion of some that this colour and the pure tortoiseshell is the original domestic cat, and that the other varieties of marking and colours are but deviations produced by crossing with wild varieties. My brother, John Jenner Weir, F.L.S., F.Z.S., holds somewhat to this opinion; but, to me, it is rather difficult to arrive at this conclusion. In fact, I can scarcely realise the ground on which the theory is based—at the same time, I do not mean to ignore it entirely. And yet, if this be so, from what starting-point was the original domestic cat derived, and by what means were the rich and varied markings obtained? I am fully aware that by selection cats with large patches of colour may be obtained; still, there remain the peculiar markings of the tortoiseshell. Nor is this by any means an uncommon colour, not only in this country, but in many others, and there also appears to be a peculiar fixedness of this, especially in the female, but why it is not so in the male I am at a loss to understand, the males almost invariably coming either red-tabby or red-tabby-and-white. One would suppose that black or white would be equally likely; but, as far as my observations take me, this is not so, though I have seen both pure white, yellow, red, and black in litters of kittens, but this might be different were the he parent tortoiseshell.

Some years ago I was out with a shooting party not far from Snowdon, in Wales, when turning past a large rock I came on a sheltered nook, and there in a nest made of dry grasses laid six tortoiseshell-and-white kittens about eight to ten days old. I was much surprised at this, as I did not know of any house near, therefore these must have been the offspring of some cat or cats that were leading a roving or wild life, and yet it had no effect as to the deviation of the colour. I left them there, and without observing the sex. I was afterwards sorry, as it is just possible, though scarcely probable, that one or more of the six, being all of the same colour, might have proved to be a male. As I left the neighbourhood a few days after I saw no more of them, nor have I since heard of any being there; so conclude they in some way were destroyed.

I have observed in the breed of tortoiseshell or tortoise-shell-and-white that the hair is of a coarser texture than the ordinary domestic cat, and that the tail is generally thicker, especially at the base, though some few are thin-tailed; yet I prefer the thick and tapering form. Some are very much so, and of a good length; the legs are generally somewhat short; I do not ever remember seeing a really long-legged tortoiseshell, though when this is so if not too long it adds much to its grace of action. I give a drawing of what I consider to be a GOOD tortoiseshell-and-white tom or he-cat. It will be observed that there is more white on the chest, belly, and hind legs than is allowable in the black-and-white cat. This I deem necessary for artistic beauty, when the colour is laid on in *patches*, although it should be even, clear, and distinct in its outline; the larger space of white adds brilliancy to the red, yellow, and black colouring. The face is one of the parts which should have some uniformity of colour, and yet not so, but a mere *balancing* of colour; that is to say, that there should be a *relief* in black, with the yellow and red on each side, and so in the body and tail. The nose should be white, the eyes orange, and the whole colouring rich and varied without the least *Tabbyness*, either brown or gray or an approach to it, such being highly detrimental to its beauty.

I have received a welcome letter from Mr. Herbert Young, of James Street, Harrogate, informing me of the existence of what is said to be a tortoiseshell tom or he-cat somewhere in Yorkshire, and the price is fifty guineas; but he, unfortunately, has forgotten the exact address. He also kindly favours me with the further information of a tortoiseshell-and-white he-cat. He describes it as "splendid," and "extra good in colour," and it is at present in the vicinity of Harrogate. And still further, Mr. Herbert Young says, "I am breeding from a dark colour cat and two tortoiseshell females," and he hopes, by careful selection, to succeed in "breeding the other colour out." This, I deem, is by no means an unlikely thing to happen, and, by careful management, may not take very long to accomplish; but much depends on the ancestry, or rather the pedigree of both sides. I for one most heartily wish Mr. Herbert Young success, and it will be most gratifying should he arrive at the height of his expectations. Failing the producing of the desired colour in the he-cats by the legitimate method of tortoiseshell with tortoiseshell, I would advise the trial of some *whole* colours, such as solid black and white. This *may* prove a better way than the other, as we pigeon fanciers go an apparently roundabout way often to obtain what we want to attain in colour, and yet there is almost a certainty in the method.

As regards the tortoiseshell cat, there is a distinct variety known to us cat fanciers as the tortoiseshell-tabby. This must not be confounded with the true variety, as it consists only of a variegation in colour of the yellow, the red, and the dark tabby, and is more in lines than patches, or patches of lines or spots. These are by no means ugly, and a well-marked, richly-coloured specimen is really very handsome. They may also be intermixed with white, and should be marked the same as the true tortoiseshell; but in competition with the *real* tortoiseshell they would stand *no chance* whatever, and ought in my opinion to be disqualified as being wrong class, and be put in that for "any other colour."

Mrs. Vyvyan's Royal Cat Of Siam.

Brown Tabby—Bars the right width.

THE BROWN TABBY CAT

The tabby cat is doubtless one of, if not the most common of colours, and numbers many almost endless varieties of both tint and markings. Of these those with very broad bands of black, or narrow bands of black, on nearly a black ground, are usually called black tabby, and if the bands are divided into spots instead of being in continuous lines, then it is a spotted black tabby; but I purpose in this paper to deal mostly with the brown tabby—that is to say, a tabby, whose ground colour is of a very rich, orangey, dark brown ground, without any white, and that is evenly, proportionably, and not too broadly but elegantly marked on the face, head, breast, sides, back, belly, legs, and tail with bands of solid, deep, shining black. The front part of the head or face and legs, breast, and belly should have a more rich red orange tint than the back, but which should be nearly if not equal in depth of colour, though somewhat browner; the markings should be graceful in curve, sharply, well, and clearly defined, with fine deep black edges, so that the brown and black are clear and distinct the one from the other, not blurred in any way. The banded tabby should not be spotted in any way, excepting those few that nearly always occur on the face and sometimes on the fore-legs. The clearer, redder, and brighter the brown the better. The nose should be deep red, bordered with black; the eyes an orange colour, slightly diffused with green; in form the head should not be large, nor too wide, being rather longer than broad, so as not to give too round or clumsy an appearance; ears not large nor small, but of moderate size, and of good form; legs medium length, rather long than short, so as not to lose grace of action; body long, narrow, and deep towards the fore part. Tail long, and gradually tapering towards the point; feet round, with black claws, and black pads; yellowish-white around the black lips and brown whiskers are allowable, but orange-tinted are far preferable, and pure white should disqualify. A cat of this description is now somewhat rare. What are generally shown as *brown* tabbies are not sufficiently *orange-brown*, but mostly of a dark, brownish-gray. This is simply the ordinary tabby, and not the *brown* tabby proper.

Brown Tabby—Markings much too wide.

As I stated in my notes on the Tortoiseshell cat, the best parents to obtain a good brown tabby from is to have a strongly marked, not too broad-banded tabby he-cat and a tortoiseshell she-cat with little black, or red tabby she-cat, the produce being, when tabby, generally of a rich brown, or sometimes what is termed black tabby, and also red tabby. The picture illustrating these notes is from one so bred, and is a particularly handsome specimen. There were two he-cats in the litter, one the dark-brown tabby just mentioned, which I named Aaron, and the other, a very fine red tabby, Moses. This last was even a finer animal than Aaron, being very beautiful in colour and very large in size; but he, alas! like many others, was caught in wires set by poachers, and was found dead. His handsome brother still survives, though no longer my property. The banded red tabby should be marked precisely the same as the brown tabby, only the bands should be of deep red on an orange ground, the deeper in colour the better; almost a chocolate on orange is very fine. The nose deep pink, as also the pads of the feet. The ordinary dark tabby the same way as the brown, and so also the blue or silver, only the ground colour should be of a pale, soft, *blue* colour—not the slightest tint of brown in it. The clearer, the *lighter*, and brighter the blue the better, bearing in mind always that the bands should be of a *jet black*, sharply and *very clearly defined.*

Well-marked prize silver tabby.

The word tabby was derived from a kind of taffeta, or ribbed silk, which when calendered or what is now termed "watered," is by that process covered with wavy lines. This stuff, in bygone times, was often called "tabby:" hence the cat with lines or markings on its fur was called a "tabby" cat. But it might also, one would suppose, with as much justice, be called a taffety cat, unless the calendering of "taffety" caused it to become "tabby." Certain it is that the word tabby only referred to the marking or stripes, not to the absolute colour, for in "Wit and Drollery" (1682), p. 343, is the following:—

"Her petticoat of satin,Her gown of crimson tabby."

Be that as it may, I think there is little doubt that the foregoing was the origin of the term. Yet it was also called the brinded cat, or the brindled cat, also tiger cat, with some the gray cat, graymalkin; but I was rather unprepared to learn that in Norfolk and Suffolk it is called a Cyprus cat. "Why Cyprus cat?" quoth I. "I do not know," said my informant. "All I know is, that such is the case."

So I referred to my Bailey's Dictionary of 1730, and there, "sure enough," was the elucidation; for I found that Cyprus was a kind of cloth made of silk and hair, showing wavy lines on it, and coming from Cyprus; therefore this somewhat strengthens the argument in favour of "taffeta," or "tabby," but it is still curious that the Norfolk and Suffolk people should have adopted a kind of cloth as that representing the markings and colour of the cat, and that of a different name from that in use for the cat—one or more counties calling it a "tabby cat," as regards colour, and the other naming the same as "Cyprus." I take this to be exceedingly interesting. How or when such naming took place I am at present unable to get the least clue, though I think from what I gather from one of the Crystal Palace Cat Show catalogues, that it must have been after 1597, as the excerpt shows that at that time the shape and colour was like a leopard's, which, of course, is spotted, and is always called the spotted leopard. (Since this I have learned that the domestic cat is said to have been brought from Cyprus by merchants, as also was the tortoiseshell. Cyprus is a colour, a sort of reddish-yellow, something like citron; so a Cyprus cat may mean a red or yellow tabby.)

However, I find Holloway, in his "Dictionary of Provincialisms" (1839), gives the following:—

"Calimanco Cat, s. (calimanco, a glossy stuff), a tortoiseshell cat, Norfolk."

Salmon, in "The Compleat English Physician," 1693, p. 326, writing of the cat, says: "It is a neat and cleanly creature, often licking itself to keep it fair and clean, and washing its face with its fore feet; the best are such as of a fair and large kind and of an exquisite tabby color called *Cyprus* cats."

SPOTTED TABBY CAT

I have thought it best to give two illustrations of the peculiar markings of the *spotted* tabby, or leopard cat of some, as showing its distinctness from the ordinary and banded Tabby, one of my reasons being that I have, when judging at cat shows, often found excellent specimens of both entered in the "wrong class," thereby losing all chance of a prize, though, if rightly entered, either might very possibly have taken honours. I therefore wish to direct particular attention to the *spotted* character of the markings of the variety called the "spotted tabby." It will be observed that there are no lines, but what are lines in other tabbies are broken up into a number of spots, and the more these spots prevail, to the exclusion of *lines* or *bands*, the better the specimen is considered to be. The varieties of the ground colour or tint on which these markings or spots are placed constitutes the name, such as black-spotted tabby, brown-spotted tabby, and so on, the red-spotted tabby or yellow-spotted tabby in *she*-cats being by far the most scarce. These should be marked with *spots* instead of *bands*, on the same ground colour as the red or yellow-banded tabby cat. In the former the ground colour should be a rich red, with spots of a deep, almost chocolate colour, while that of the yellow tabby may be a deep yellow cream, with yellowish-brown spots. Both are very scarce, and are extremely pretty. Any admixture of white is not allowable in the class for yellow or red tabbies; such exhibit must be put into the class (should there be one, which is usually the case at large shows) for red or yellow and *white* tabbies. This exhibitors will do well to make a note of.

There is a rich-coloured brown tabby hybrid to be seen at the Zoological Society Gardens in Regent's Park, between the wild cat of Bengal and a tabby shc-cat. It is handsome, but very wild.

83

These hybrids, I am told, will breed again with tame variety, or with others.

In the brown-spotted tabby, the dark gray-spotted tabby, the black-spotted tabby, the gray or the blue-spotted tabby, the eyes are best yellow or orange tinted, with the less of the green the better. The nose should be of a dark red, edged with black or dark brown, in the dark colours, or somewhat lighter colour in the gray or blue tabbies. The pads of the feet in all instances must be black. In the yellow and the red tabby the nose and the pads of the feet are to be pink. As regards the tail, that should have large spots on the upper and lower sides instead of being annulated, but this is difficult to obtain. It has always occurred to me that the spotted tabby is a much nearer approach to the wild English cat and some other wild cats in the way of colour than the ordinary broad-banded tabby. Those specimens of the crosses, said to be between the wild and domestic cat, that I have seen, have had a tendency to be spotted tabbies. And these crosses were not infrequent in bygone times when the wild cats were more numerous than at present, as is stated to be the case by that reliable authority, Thomas Bewick. In the year 1873, there was a specimen shown at the Crystal Palace Cat Show, and also the last year or two there has been exhibited at the same place a most beautiful hybrid between the East Indian wild cat and the domestic cat. It was shown in the spotted tabby class, and won the first prize. The ground colour was a deep blackish-brown, with well-defined black spots, black pads to the feet, rich in colour, and very strong and powerfully made, and not by any means a sweet temper. It was a he-cat, and though I have made inquiry, I have not been able to ascertain that any progeny has been reared from it, yet I have been informed that such hybrids between the Indian wild cat and the domestic cat breed freely.

THE ABYSSINIAN

I now come to the last variety of the tabby cat, and this can scarcely be called a tabby proper, as it is nearly destitute of markings, excepting sometimes on the legs and a broad black band along the back. It is mostly of a deep brown, ticked with black, somewhat resembling the back of a wild (only not so gray) rabbit. Along the centre of the back, from the nape of the neck to the tip of the tail, there is a band of black, very slightly interspersed with dark brown hairs. The inner sides of the legs and belly are more of a rufous-orange tint than the body, and are marked in some cases with a few dark patches; but they are best without these marks, and in the exhibition pens it is a point lost. The eyes are deep yellow, tinted with green; nose dark red, black-edged; ears rather small, dark brown, with black edges and tips; the pads of the feet are black. Altogether, it is a pretty and interesting variety. It has been shown under a variety of names, such as Russian, Spanish, Abyssinian, Hare cat, Rabbit cat, and some have gone so far as to maintain that it is a cross between the latter and a cat, proving very unmistakably there is nothing, however absurd or impossible, in animal or everyday life, that some people are not ready to credit and believe. A hybrid between the English wild cat and the domestic much resembles it; and I do not consider it different in any way, with the exception of its colour, from the ordinary tabby cat, from which I have seen kittens and adults bearing almost the same appearance. Some years ago when out rabbit-shooting on the South Downs, not far from Eastbourne, one of our party shot a cat of this colour in a copse not far from the village of Eastdean. He mistook it at first for a rabbit as it dashed into the underwood. It proved not to be wild, but belonged to one of the villagers, and was bred in the village. When the ground colour is light gray or blue, it is generally called chinchilla, to the fur of which animal the coat has a general resemblance. I have but little inclination to place it as a distinct, though often it is of foreign breed; such may be, though ours is merely a variety—and a very interesting one— of the ordinary tabby, with which its form, habits, temper, etc., seem fully to correspond; still several have been imported from Abyssinia all of which were precisely similar, and it is stated that this is the origin of the Egyptian cat that was worshipped so many centuries ago. The mummies of the cats I have seen in no case had any hair left, so that it was impossible to determine what colour they were. The imported cats are of stouter build than the English and less marked. These bred with an English tabby often give a result of nearly black, the back band extending very much down the sides, and the brown ticks almost disappearing, producing a rich and beautiful colouring.

I find there is yet another tint or colour of the tabby proper which I have not mentioned, that is to say, a cat marked with light wavy lines, and an exceedingly pretty one it is. It is very rare; in fact, so much so that it has never had a class appropriated to it, and therefore is only admissible to or likely to win in the class "For Any Other Colour," in which class usually a number of very beautiful varieties are to be found, some of which I shall have occasion to notice further on. The colour, however, that I now refer to is often called the silver tabby, for want of a better name. It is this. The whole of the ground colour is of a most delicate silver-gray, clear and firm in tone, slightly blue if anything apart from the gray, and the markings thereon are but a little darker, with a tinge of lilac in them making the fur to look like an evening sky, rayed with light clouds. The eyes are orange-yellow, and when large and full make a fine contrast to the colour of the fur. The nose is red, edged with a lilac tint, and the pads of the feet and claws are black, or nearly so. The hair is generally very fine, short, and soft. Altogether it is most lovely, and well worthy of attention, forming, as it does, a beautiful contrast to the red, the yellow, or even the brown tabby. A turquoise ribbon about its neck will show to great advantage the delicate lilac tints of its coat, or, if a contrast is preferred, a light orange scarlet, or what is often called geranium colour, will perhaps give a brighter and more pleasing effect.

Mrs. Herring's blue small-banded Tabby.

This is by no means so uncommon a colour in the *long-haired* cats, some of which are exquisite, and are certainly the acme of beauty in the way of cat colouring; but I must here remark that there is a vast difference in the way of disposition between these two light varieties, that of the former being far more gentle. In fact, I am of opinion that the short-haired cat in general is of a more genial temperament, more "cossetty," more observant, more quick in adapting itself to its surroundings and circumstances than its long-haired brother, and, as a rule, it is also more cleanly in its habits. Though at the same time I am willing to admit that some of these peculiarities being set aside, the long-haired cat is charmingly beautiful, and at the same time has a large degree of intelligence—in fact, much more than most animals that I know, not even setting aside the dog, and I have come to this conclusion after much long, careful, and mature consideration.

THE SHORT-HAIRED WHITE CAT

This of all, as it depends entirely on its comeliness, should be graceful and elegant in the outline of its form and also action, the head small, not too round nor thick, for this gives a clumsy, heavy appearance, but broad on the forehead, and gently tapering towards the muzzle, the nose small, tip even and pink, the ears rather small than large, and not too pointed, the neck slender, shoulders narrow and sloping backwards, loin full and long, legs of moderate length, tail well set on, long, broad at the base, and gradually tapering towards the end; the white should be the yellow-white, that is, the white of the colours, such as tortoiseshell, red tabby or blues, not the gray-white bred from the black, as these are coarser in the quality of the furs. The eye should be large, round, full, and blue. I noted this peculiarity of white when breeding white Cochins many years ago; those chickens that were black when hatched were a colder and harder white than those which were hatched buff. This colouring of white should be fully borne in mind when crossing colours in breeding, as the results are widely different from the two varieties. The whole colour yellow-white will not do to match with blue or gray, as it will assuredly give the wrong tinge or colour.

The eyes should be blue; green is a great defect; bright yellow is allowable, or what in horses is called "wall eyes." Orange gives a heavy appearance; but yellow will harmonise and look well with a gray-white.

White cats with blue eyes are hardy. Mr. Timbs, in "Things Not Generally Known," relates that even they are not so likely to be deaf as is supposed, and mentions one of seventeen years old which retained its hearing faculties perfectly. Some specimens I have seen with one yellow eye and one blue; this is a most singular freak of nature, and to the best of my knowledge is not to be found among any of the other colours.

It is stated that one of the white horses recently presented by the Shah of Persia to the Emperor of Russia has blue eyes. I can scarcely credit this, but think it must be a true albino, with the gray-pink coloured eyes they generally have, or possibly the blue eye is that peculiar to the *albino* cat and horse, as I have never seen an albino horse or cat with pink eyes but a kind of opalesque colour, or what is termed "wall eye." No doubt many of my readers have observed the differences in the white of our horses, they mostly being the gray-white, with dark skin; but the purer white has a pink skin, and is much softer and elegant in appearance. It is the same with our white cats.

THE BLACK CAT

It is often said "What's in a name?" the object, whatever it is, by any other would be the same, and yet there is much in a name; but this is not the question at issue, which is that of colour. Why should a *black* cat be thought so widely different from all others by the foolish, unthinking, and ignorant? Why, simply on account of its colour being black, should it have ascribed to it a numberless variety of bad omens, besides having certain necromantic power? In Germany, for instance, black cats are kept away from children as omens of evil, and if a black cat appeared in the room of one lying ill it was said to portend death. To meet a black cat in the twilight was held unlucky. In the "good old times" a black cat was generally the only colour that was favoured by men reported to be wizards, and also were said to be the constant companions of reputed witches, and in such horror and detestation were they then held that when the unfortunate creatures were ill-treated, drowned, or even burned, very frequently we are told that their cats suffered martyrdom at the same time. It is possible that one of the reasons for such wild, savage superstition may have arisen from the fact of the larger amount of electricity to be found by friction in the coat of the black cat to any other; experiments prove there is but very little either in that of the white or the red tabby cat. Be this as it may, still the fact remains that, for some reason or other, the black cat is held by the prejudiced ignorant as an animal most foul and detestable, and wonderful stories are related of their actions in the dead of the night during thunder-storms and windy nights. Yet, as far as I can discover, there appears little difference either of temper or habit in the black cat distinct from that of any other colour, though it is maintained by many even to this day that black cats are far more vicious and spiteful and of higher courage, and this last I admit. Still, when a black cat is enraged and its coat and tail are well "set up," its form swollen, its round, bright, orange-yellow eye distended and all aglow with anger, it certainly presents to even the most impartial observer, to say the least of it, a most "uncanny" appearance. But, for all this, their admirers are by no means few; and, to my thinking, a jet-black cat, fine and glossy in fur and elegantly formed, certainly has its attractions; but I will refer to the superstitions connected with the black cat further on.

A black cat for show purposes should be of a uniform, intense black; a brown-black is richer than a blue-black. I mean by this that when the hair is parted it should show in the division a dark brown-black in preference to any tint of blue whatever. The coat or fur should be short, velvety, and very glossy. The eyes round and full, and of a deep orange colour; nose black, and also the pads of the feet; tail long, wide at the base, and tapering gradually towards the end. A long thin tail is a great fault, and detracts much from the merits it may otherwise possess. A good, deep, rich-coloured black cat is not so common as many may at first suppose, as often those that are said to be black show tabby markings under certain conditions of light; and, again, others want depth and richness of colour, some being only a very dark gray. In form it is the same as other short-haired cats, such as I have described in the white, and this brings me to the variety called "blue."

Archangel Blue Cat.

THE BLUE CAT

This is shown often under a number of names. It was at first shown as the Archangel cat, then Russian blue, Spanish blue, Chartreuse blue, and, lastly, and I know not why, the American blue. It is not, in my belief, a distinct breed, but merely a light-coloured form of the black cat. In fact, I have ascertained that one shown at the Crystal Palace, and which won many prizes on account of its beautiful blue colour slightly tinged with purple, was the offspring of a tabby and white she-cat and a black-and-white he-cat, and I have seen the same colour occur when bred from the cats usually kept about a farmhouse as a protection from rats and mice, though none of the parents had any blue colour.

Being so beautiful, and as it is possible in some places abroad it may be bred in numbers, I deemed it advisable, when making out the prize schedule, to give special prizes for this colour; the fur being used for various purposes on account of its hue. A fine specimen should be even in colour, of a bluish-lilac tint, with no sootiness or black, and though light be firm and rich in tone, the nose and pads dark, and the eyes orange-yellow. If of a very light blue-gray, the nose and pads may be of a deep chocolate colour and the eyes deep yellow, not green. If it is a foreign variety, I can only say that I see no distinction in form, temper, or habit; and, as I have before mentioned, it is sometimes bred here in England from cats bearing no resemblance to the bluish-lilac colour, nor of foreign extraction or pedigree. I feel bound, however, to admit that those that came from Archangel were of a deeper, purer tint than the English cross-breeds; and on reference to my notes, I find they had larger ears and eyes, and were larger and longer in the head and legs, also the coat or fur was excessively short, rather inclined to woolliness, but bright and glossy, the hair inside the ears being shorter than is usual in the English cat.

THE BLACK-AND-WHITE CAT

This is distinct from the *white-and-black* cat, the ground colour being black, marked with white; while the other is white, marked with black. The chief points of excellence for show purposes are a dense bright brown-black, evenly marked with white. Of this I give an illustration, showing the most approved way in which the white should be distributed, coming to a point between the eyes. The feet should be white, and the chest, the nose, and the pads white. No black on the lips or nose, whiskers white, eyes of orange yellow. Any black on the white portions is highly detrimental to its beauty and its chance of a prize.

The same markings are applicable to the brown tabby and white, the dark tabby and white, the red tabby and white, the yellow tabby and white, the blue or silver tabby and white, and the blue and white. One great point is to obtain a perfectly clear and distinct gracefully-curved outline of colour, and this to be maintained throughout; the blaze on the forehead to be central. It is stated that if a dog has white anywhere, he is sure to have a white tip to his tail, and I think, on observation, it will be found usually the case, although this is not so in the cat, for I cannot call to mind a single instance where a black-and-white had a white tip to its tail; but taking the various colours of the domestic cat into consideration I think it will be found that there is a larger number with some white about them than those of entirely one colour, without even a few white hairs, which if they appear at all are mostly to be found on the chest, though they often are exceedingly few in number.

Mrs. Vyvyan's Royal Cat Of Siam.

THE WHITE-AND-BLACK CAT

This differs entirely from the black-and-white cat, as just explained, and is the opposite as regards colour, the ground being white instead of black, and the markings black on white. For exhibition purposes and points of excellence, no particular rule exists beyond that the exhibit shall be evenly marked, with the colour distributed so as to balance, as, for example:—If a cat has a black patch just *under* one eye with a *little above*, the balance of colour would be maintained if the other eye had a preponderance of colour *above* instead of *below*, and so with the nose, shoulders, or back, but it would be far better if the patches of colour were the same size and shape, and equal in position. It might be that a cat evenly marked on the head had a mark on the left shoulder with more on the right, with a rather larger patch on the right side of the loin, or a black tail would help considerably to produce what is termed "*balance*," though a cat of this description would lose if competing against one of entirely uniform markings.

I have seen several that have been marked in a very singular way. One was entirely white, with black ears. Another white, with a black tail only. This had orange eyes, and was very pretty. Another had a black blaze up the nose, the rest of the animal being white. This had blue eyes, and was deaf. Another had the two front feet black, all else being white; the eyes were yellow-tinted green. All these, it will be observed, were perfect in the way they were marked.

I give an illustration of a cat belonging to Mr. S. Lyon, of Crewe. It is remarkable in more ways than one, and in all probability, had it been born in "the dark ages" a vast degree of importance would have been attached to it, not only on account

100

of the peculiar distribution of the colour and its form, but also as to the singular coincidence of its birth. The head is white, with a black mark over the eyes and ears which, when looked at from above, presents the appearance of a *fleur-de-lis*. The body is white, with a distinct black cross on the right side, or, rather, more on the back than side. The cross resembles that known as Maltese in form, and is clearly defined. The tail is black, the legs and feet white. Nor does the cat's claim to notice entirely end here, for, marvellous to relate, it was born on Easter Sunday, A.D. 1886. Now, what would have been said of such a coincidence had this peculiar development of Nature occurred in bygone times? There is just the possibility that the credulous would have "flocked" to see the wondrous animal from far and near; and even now, in these enlightened times, I learn from Mr. Lyon that the cat is not by any means devoid of interest and attraction, for, as he tells me, a number of persons have been to see it, some of whom predict that "luck" will follow, and that he and his household will, in consequence, *doubtless* enjoy many blessings, and that all things will prosper with him accordingly.

Although my remarks are directed to "the white-and-black" cat, the same will apply to the "white-and-red, white-and-yellow, white-and-tabby, white-and-blue, or dun colour;" all these, and the foregoing, will most probably have to be exhibited in the "Any Other Colour" class, as there is seldom one at even the largest shows for peculiar markings with white as the *ground* or principal colour.

SIAMESE CAT

Among the beautiful varieties of the domestic cat brought into notice by the cat shows, none deserve more attention than "The Royal Cat of Siam." In form, colour, texture, and length, or rather shortness of its coat, it is widely different from other short-haired varieties; yet there is but little difference in its mode of life or habit. I have not had the pleasure of owning one of this breed, though when on a visit to Lady Dorothy Nevill, at Dangstein, near Petersfield, I had several opportunities for observation. I noticed in particular the intense liking of these cats for "the woods," not passing along the hedgerows like the ordinary cat, but quickly and quietly creeping from bush to bush, then away in the shaws; not that they displayed a wildness of nature, in being shy or distrustful, nor did they seem to care about getting wet like many cats do, though apparently they suffer much when it is cold and damp weather, as would be likely on account of the extreme shortness of their fur, which is of both a hairy and a woolly texture, and not so glossy as our ordinary common domestic cat, nor is the tail, which is thin. Lady Dorothy Nevill informed me that those which belonged to her were imported from Siam and presented by Sir R. Herbert of the Colonial Office; the late Duke of Wellington imported the breed, also Mr. Scott of Rotherfield. Lady Dorothy Nevill thought them exceedingly docile and domestic, but delicate in their constitution; although her ladyship kept one for two years, another over a year, but eventually all died of the same complaint, that of worms, which permeated every part of their body.

Mr. Young, of Harrogate, possesses a chocolate variety of this Royal Siamese cat; it was sent from Singapore to Mr. Brennand, from whom he purchased it, and is described as "most loving and affectionate," which I believe is usually the case. Although this peculiar colour is very beautiful and scarce, I am of opinion that the light gray or fawn colour with black and well-marked muzzle, ears, and legs is the typical variety, the markings being the same as the Himalayan rabbits. There are cavies so marked; and many years ago I saw a mouse similarly coloured. Mr. Young informs me that the kittens he has bred from his dark variety have invariably come the usual gray or light dun colour with dark points. I therefore take that to be the correct form and colour, and the darker colour to be an accidental deviation. In pug-dogs such a depth of colour would be considered a blemish, however beautiful it might be; even black pugs do not obtain prizes in competition with a true-marked light dun; but whatever colour the body is it should be clear and firm, rich and not clouded in any way. But I give Mr. Young's own views:

"The dun Siamese we have has won whenever shown; the body is of a dun colour, nose, part of the face, ears, feet, and tail of a very dark chocolate brown, nearly black, eyes of a beautiful blue by day, and of a red colour at night! My other prize cat is of a very rich chocolate or seal, with darker face, ears, and tail; the legs are a shade darker, which intensifies towards the feet. The eyes small, of a rich amber colour, the ears are bare of hair, and not so much hair between the eyes and the ears as the English cats have. The dun, unless under special judges, invariably beats the chocolate at the shows. The tail is shorter and finer than our English cats.

"I may add that we lately have had four kittens from the chocolate cat by a pure dun Siamese he-cat. All the young are dun coloured, and when born were very light, nearly white, but are gradually getting the dark points of the parents; in fact, I expect that one will turn chocolate. The cats are very affectionate, and make charming ladies' pets, but are rather more delicate than our cats, but after they have once wintered in England they seem to get acclimatised.

"Mr. Brennand, who brought the chocolate one and another, a male, from Singapore last year, informs me that there are two varieties, a large and small. Ours are the small; he also tells me the chocolate is the most rare.

"I have heard a little more regarding the Siamese cats from Miss Walker, the daughter of General Walker, who brought over one male and three females. It seems the only pure breed is kept at the King of Siam's palace, and the cats are very difficult to procure, for in Siam it took three different gentlemen of great influence three months before they could get any.

"Their food is fish and rice boiled together until quite soft, and Miss Walker finds the kittens bred have thriven on it.

"It is my intention to try and breed from a white English female with blue eyes, and a Siamese male.

"The Siamese cats are very prolific breeders, having generally five at each litter, and three litters a year.

"We have never succeeded in breeding any like our chocolate cat; they all come fawn, with black or dark brown points; the last family are a little darker on their backs, which gives them a richer appearance than the pale fawn. Hitherto we have never had any half-bred Siamese; but there used to be a male Siamese at Hurworth-on-Tees, and there were many young bred from English cats. They invariably showed the Siamese cross in the ground colour."

From the foregoing it will be seen how very difficult it is to obtain the pure breed, even in Siam, and on reference to the Crystal Palace catalogues from the year 1871 until 1887, I find that there were *fifteen* females and only *four* males, and some of these were not entire; and I have always understood that the latter were not allowed to be exported, and were only got by those so fortunate as a most extraordinary favour, as the King of Siam is most jealous of keeping the breed entirely in Siam as royal cats.

The one exhibited by Lady Dorothy Nevill (Mrs. Poodle) had three kittens by an English cat; but none showed any trace of the Siamese, being all tabby.

Although Mr. Herbert Young was informed by Mr. Brennand that there is another and a larger breed in Siam, it does not appear that any of these have been imported; nor have we any description of them, either as to colour, size, form, or quality of coat, or whether they resemble the lesser variety in this or any respect, yet it is to be hoped that, ere long, some specimens may be secured for this country.

Besides Mr. Herbert Young, I am also much indebted to the courtesy of Mrs. Vyvyan, of Dover, who is a lover of this beautiful breed, and who kindly sends the following information:

"The original pair were sent from Bangkok, and it is believed that they came from the King's Palace, where alone the breed are said to be kept pure. At any rate they were procured as a great favour, after much delay and great difficulty, and since that time no others have been attainable by the same person. We were in China when they reached us, and the following year, 1886, we brought the father, mother, and a pair of kittens to England.

"Their habits are in general the same as the common cat, though it has been observed by strangers, 'there is a pleasant wild animal odour,' which is not apparent to us.

"Most of the kittens have a kink in the tail; it varies in position, sometimes in the middle, close to the body, or at the extreme end like a hook."

This tallies with the description given by Mr. Darwin of the Malayan and also the Siamese cats. See my notes on the Manx cat. Mr. Young had also noted this peculiarity in "the Royal cat of Siam."

Mrs. Vyvyan further remarks:

"They are very affectionate and personally attached to their human friends, not liking to be left alone, and following us from room to room more after the manner of dogs than cats.

"They are devoted parents, the old father taking the greatest interest in the young ones.

"They are friendly with the dogs of the house, occupying the same baskets; but the males are very strong, and fight with great persistency with strange dogs, and conquer all other tom-cats in their neighbourhood. We lost one, however, a very fine cat, in China in this way, as he returned to the house almost torn to pieces and in a dying condition, from an encounter with some animal which we think was one of the wild cats of the hills.

"We feed them on fresh fish boiled with rice, until the two are nearly amalgamated; they also take bread and milk *warm*, the milk having been boiled, and this diet seems to suit them better than any other. They also like chicken and game. We have proved the fish diet is not essential, as two of our cats (in Cornwall) never get it.

"Rather a free life seems necessary to their perfect acclimatisation, where they can go out and provide themselves with raw animal food, 'feather and fur.'

"We find these cats require a great deal of care, unless they live in the country, and become hardy through being constantly out of doors. The kittens are difficult to rear unless they are born late in the spring, thus having the warm weather before them. Most deaths occur before they are six months old.

"We have lost several kittens from worms, which they endeavour to vomit; as relief we give them raw chicken heads, with *the feathers on*, with success. We also give cod-liver oil, if the appetite fails and weight diminishes.

"When first born the colour is nearly pure white, the only trace of 'points' being a fine line of dark gray at the edge of the ears; a gradual alteration takes place, the body becoming creamy, the ears, face, tail, and feet darkening, until, about a year old, they attain perfection, when the points should be the deepest brown, nearly black, and the body ash or fawn colour, eyes opal or blue, looking red in the dark. After maturity they are apt to darken considerably, though not in all specimens.

"They are most interesting and delightful pets. But owing to their delicacy and the great care they require, no one, unless a real cat *lover*, should attempt to keep them; they cannot with safety to their health be treated as common cats.

"During 'Susan's' (one of the cats) illness, the old he-cat came daily to condole with her, bringing delicate 'attentions' in the form of freshly-caught mice. 'Loquat' also provided this for a young family for whom she had no milk.

"Another, 'Saiwan,' is very clever at undoing the latch of the window in order to let himself out; tying it up with string is of no use, and he has even managed to untwist wire that has been used to prevent his going out in the snow. We have at present two males, four adult females, and five kittens." One of our kittens sent to Scotland last August, has done well.

Mrs. Lee, of Penshurst, also has some fine specimens of the breed, and of the same colours as described. I take it, therefore, that the true breed, by consensus of opinion, is that of the dun, fawn, or ash-coloured ground, with black points. Other colours should be shown in the variety classes.

The head should be long from the ears to the eyes, and not over broad, and then rather sharply taper off towards the muzzle, the forehead flat, and receding, the eyes somewhat aslant downwards towards the nose, and the eyes of a pearly, yet bright blue colour, the ears usual size and black, with little or no hair on the inside, with black muzzle, and round the eyes black. The form should be slight, graceful, and delicately made, body long, tail rather short and thin, and the legs somewhat short, slender, and the feet oval, not so round as the ordinary English cat. The body should be one bright, uniform, even colour, not clouded, either rich fawn, dun, or ash. The legs, feet, and tail black. The back slightly darker is allowable, if of a rich colour, and the colour softened, *not clouded*.

Properly marked Siamese cat.

THE MANX CAT

The Manx cat is well known, and is by no means uncommon. It differs chiefly from the ordinary domestic cat in being tailless, or nearly so, the best breeds not having any; the hind legs are thicker and rather longer, particularly in the thighs. It runs more like a hare than a cat, the action of the legs being awkward, nor does it seem to turn itself so readily, or with such rapidity and ease; the head is somewhat small for its size, yet thick and well set on a rather long neck; the eyes large, round, and full, ears medium, and rather rounded at the apex. In colour they vary, but I do not remember to have seen a white or many black, though one of the best that has come under my notice was the latter colour. I have examined a number of specimens sent for exhibition at the Crystal Palace and other cat shows, and found in some a very short, thin, twisted tail, in others a mere excrescence, and some with an appendage more like a knob. These I have taken as having been operated upon when young, the tail being removed, but this may not be the case, as Mr. St. George Mivart in his very valuable book on the cat, mentions a case where a female cat had her tail so injured by the passage of a cart-wheel over it, that her master judged it best to have it cut off near the base. Since then she has had two litters of kittens, and in each litter one or more of the kittens had a *stump of tail*, while their brothers and sisters had tails of the usual length. But were there no Manx cats in the neighbourhood, is a query. This case is analogous to the statement that the short-tailed sheep-dog was produced from parents that had had their tails amputated; and yet this is now an established breed. Also a small black breed of dogs from the Netherlands, which is now very fashionable. They are called "Chipperkes," and have no tails, at least when

111

exhibited. Mr. St. George Mivart further states that Mr. Bartlett told him, as he has so stated to myself, that in the Isle of Man the cats have tails of different lengths, from nothing up to ten inches. I have also been informed on good authority that the Fox Terrier dogs, which invariably have (as a matter of fashion) their tails cut short, sometimes have puppies with much shorter tails than the original breed; but this does not appear to take effect on sheep, whose tails are generally cut off. I cannot, myself, come to the same conclusion as to the origin of the Manx cat. Be this as it may, one thing is certain: that cross-bred Manx with other cats often have young that are tailless. As a proof of this, Mr. Herbert Young, of Harrogate, has had in his possession a very fine red female long-haired tailless cat, that was bred between the Manx and a Persian. Another case showing the strong prepotency of the Manx cat. Mr. Hodgkin, of Eridge, some time ago had a female Manx cat sent to him. Not only does she produce tailless cats when crossed with the ordinary cat, but the progeny again crossed also frequently have some tailless kittens in each litter. I have also been told there is a breed of tailless cats in Cornwall. Mr. Darwin states in his book on "The Variation of Animals and Plants under Domestication," vol. i. p. 47, that "throughout an immense area, namely, the Malayan Archipelago, Siam, Pequan, and Burmah, all the cats have truncated tails about half the proper length, often with a sort of knob at the end." This description tallies somewhat with the appearance of some of the Siamese cats that have been imported, several of which, though they have fairly long and thin tails, and though they are much pointed at the end, often have a break or kink. In a note Mr. Darwin says, "The Madagascar cat is said to have a twisted tail." (See Desmares, in Encyclop. Nat. Mamm., 1820, p. 233, for some other breeds.) Mr. St. George Mivart also corroborates the statement, so far as the Malay cat is concerned. He says the tail is only half the ordinary length, and often contorted into a sort of knot, so that it cannot be straightened. He further states, "Its contortion is due to deformity of the bones of the tail," and there is a tailless breed of cats in the Crimea. Some of the Manx cats I have examined have precisely the kind of tail here described— thin, very short, and twisted, that cannot be straightened. Is it possible that the Manx cat originated from the Malayan? Or rather is it a freak of nature perpetuated by selection? Be this as it may, we have the Manx cat now as a distinct breed, and, when crossed with others, will almost always produce some entirely tailless kittens, if not all. Many of the Siamese kittens bred here have kinks in their tails.

The illustration I give is that of a prize winner at the Crystal Palace in 1880, 1881, 1882, and is the property of Mr. J. M. Thomas, of Parliament Street. In colour it is a brindled tortoiseshell. It is eight years old. At the end of this description I also give a portrait of one of its kittens, a tabby; both are true Manx, and neither have a particle of tail, only a very small tuft of hair which is boneless. The hind quarters are very square and deep, as contrasted with other cats, and the flank deeper, giving an appearance of great strength, the hind legs being longer, and thicker in proportion to the fore legs, which are much slighter and tapering; even the toes are smaller. The head is round for a she-cat, and the ears somewhat large and pointed, but thin and fine in the hair, the cavity of the ear has *less hair within it* (also a trait of the Siamese) than some other short-haired cats, the neck is long and thin, as are the shoulders. Its habits are the same as those of most cats. I may add that Mr. Thomas, who is an old friend of mine, has had this breed many years, and kept it perfectly pure.

VARIOUS COLOURS

Those who have had much to do with breeding, and crossing of animals, birds, or plants, well know that with time, leisure, and patience, how comparatively easy it is to improve, alter, enlarge, or diminish any of these, or any part of them; and looking at the cat from this standpoint, now that it is becoming "a fancy" animal, there is no prophesying what forms, colours, markings, or other variations will be made by those who understand what can be done by careful, well-considered matching, and skilful selection. We have now cats with no tails, short tails, and some of moderate length, long tails bushy and hairy; but should a very long tail be in request, I have no doubt whatever but that in a few years it would be produced; and now that there is a cat club constituted for the welfare and improvement of the condition, as well as the careful breeding of cats, curious and unforeseen results are most likely to be attained; but whether any will ever excel the many beautiful varieties we now have, is a problem that remains to be solved.

This concludes the numerous varieties of *colours* and the proper markings of the domestic cat, as regards beauty and the points of excellence to be observed for the purposes of exhibition. These are distinct, and as such, nearly all have classes for each individual colour and marking, and therefore it is imperative that the owner should note carefully the different properties and beauties of his or her particular specimen, and also as carefully read the schedule of prizes with such attention as to be enabled to enter his or her pet in the proper class; for, it is not only annoying to the exhibitor but to the judge to find an animal sometimes of extraordinary merit placed in the "wrong class" by *sheer inattention* to the *printed rules* and instructions prepared by the committee or promoters of the show. It is exceedingly distasteful, and I may say almost distressing, to a judge to find a splendid animal wrongly entered, and so to feel himself compelled to "pass it," and to affix the words fatal to all chance of winning—"Wrong class." Again let me impress on exhibitors to be careful—very careful—in this matter—this matter of entry—for I may say it is one of the reasons which has led to my placing these notes on paper, though I have done so with much pleasure, and with earnest hope that they will be found of some value and service to the "uninitiated."

Of course there are, as there must be, a number of beautiful shades of colour, tints, and markings that are difficult to define or describe; colours and markings that are intermediate with those noticed; but though in themselves they are extremely interesting, and even very beautiful, they do not come within the range of the classes for certain definite forms of lines, spots, or colourings, as I have endeavoured to point out, and, indeed, it was almost impossible to make a sufficient number of classes to comprehend the whole. Therefore it has been considered wisest and even necessary as the most conducive to the best interests of the exhibitor and also to simplify the difficulties of judging, and for the maintenance of the various forms of beauty of the cat, to have classes wherein they are shown under rules of colour, points of beauty and excellence that are "hard and fast," and by this means all may not only know how and in what class to exhibit, but also what their chance is of "taking honours."

As I have just stated, there are intermediate colours, markings, and forms, so extra classes have been provided for these, under the heading of "any other variety of colour," and "any other variety not before mentioned," and "any cats of peculiar structure." In this last case, the cats that have abnormal formations, such as seven toes, or even nine on their fore and hind legs, peculiar in other ways, such as three legs, or only two legs, as I have seen, may be exhibited. I regard these, however, as malformations, and not to be encouraged, being generally devoid of beauty, and lacking interest for the ordinary observer, and they also tend to create a morbid taste for the unnatural and ugly, instead of the beautiful; the beautiful, be it what it may, is always pleasant to behold; and there is but little, if any, doubt in my mind but that the constant companionship of even a beautiful cat must have a soothing effect. Therefore, not in cats only, but in all things have the finest and best. Surround yourself with the elegant, the graceful, the brilliant, the beautiful, the agile, and the gentle. Be it what it may, animal, bird, or flower, be careful to have the best. A man, it is said, is made more or less by his environments, and doubtless this is to a great extent, if not entirely, a fact; that being so, the contemplation of the beautiful must have its quieting, restful influences, and tend to a brighter and happier state of existence. I am fully aware there are many that may differ from me, though I feel sure I am not far wrong when I aver there are few animals really more beautiful than a cat. If it is a good, carefully selected specimen, well kept, well cared for, in high condition, in its prime of life, well-trained, graceful in every line, bright in colour, distinct in markings, supple and elegant in form, agile and gentle in its ways, it is beautiful to look at and must command admiration. Yes! the contemplation of the beautiful elevates the mind, if only in a cat; beauty of any kind, is beauty, and has its refining influences.

USEFULNESS OF CATS

In our urban and suburban houses what should we do without cats? In our sitting or bedrooms, our libraries, in our kitchens and storerooms, our farms, barns, and rickyards, in our docks, our granaries, our ships, and our wharves, in our corn markets, meat markets, and other places too numerous to mention, how useful they are! In our ships, however, the rats oft set them at defiance; still they are of great service.

How wonderfully patient is the cat when watching for rats or mice, awaiting their egress from their place of refuge or that which is their home! How well Shakespeare in *Pericles*, Act iii., describes this keen attention of the cat to its natural pursuit!

> The cat, with eyne of burning coal,
> Now crouches from (before) the mouse's hole.

A slight rustle, and the fugitive comes forth; a quick, sharp, resolute motion, and the cat has proved its usefulness. Let any one have a plague of rats and mice, as I once had, and let them be delivered therefrom by cats, as I was, and they will have a lasting and kind regard for them.

A friend not long since informed me that a cat at Stone's Distillery was seen to catch two rats at one time, a fore foot on each. All the cats kept at this establishment, and there are several, are of the red tabby colour, and therefore most likely all males.

I am credibly informed of a still more extraordinary feat of a cat in catching mice, that of a red tabby cat which on being taken into a granary at Sevenoaks where there were a number of mice, dashed in among a retreating group, and secured four, one with each paw and two in her mouth.

At the office of *The Morning Advertiser*, I am informed by my old friend Mr. Charles Williams, they boast of a race of cats bred there for nearly half a century. In colour these are mostly tortoiseshell, and some are very handsome.

The Government, mindful also of their utility, pay certain sums, which are regularly passed through the accounts quarterly, for the purpose of providing and keeping cats in our public offices, dockyards, stores, shipping, etc., thereby proving, if proof were wanting, their acknowledged worth.

In Vienna four cats are employed by the town magistrates to catch mice on the premises of the municipality. A regular allowance is voted for their keep, and, after a limited period of active service, they are placed on the "retired list," with a comfortable pension.

There are also a number of cats in the service of the United States Post Office. These cats are distributed over the different offices to protect the bags from being eaten by rats and mice, and the cost of providing for them is duly inscribed in the accounts. When a birth takes place, the local postmaster informs the district superintendent of the fact, and obtains an addition to his rations.

A short time ago, the budget of the Imperial Printing Office in France, amongst other items, contained one for cats, which caused some merriment in the legislative chamber during its discussion. According to the *Pays* these cats are kept for the purpose of destroying the numerous rats and mice which infest the premises, and cause considerable damage to the large stock of paper which is always stored there. This feline staff is fed twice a day, and a man is employed to look after them; so that for cats' meat and the keeper's salary no little expense is annually incurred; sufficient, in fact, to form a special item in the national expenditure.

Mr. W. M. Acworth, in his excellent book, "The Railways of England," gives a very interesting account of the usefulness of the cat. He says, writing of the Midland Railway: "A few miles further off, however—at Trent—is a still more remarkable portion of the company's staff, eight cats, who are borne on the strength of the establishment, and for whom a sufficient allowance of milk and cats' meat is provided. And when we say that the cats have under their charge, according to the season of the year, from one to three or four hundred thousand empty corn sacks, it will be admitted that the company cannot have many servants who better earn their wages.

"The holes in the sacks, which are eaten by the rats which are not killed by the cats, are darned by twelve women, who are employed by the company."

Few people know, or wish to know, what a boon to mankind is "The Domestic Cat." Liked or disliked, there is the cat, in some cases unthought of or uncared for, but simply kept on account of the devastation that would otherwise take place were rats and mice allowed to have undivided possession. An uncle of mine had some hams sent from Yorkshire; during the transit by rail the whole of the interior of one of the largest was consumed by rats. More cats at the stations would possibly have prevented such irritating damage.

And further, it is almost incredible, and likewise almost unknown, the great benefit the cat is to the farmer. All day they sleep in the barns, stables, or outhouses, among the hay or straw. At eve they are seen about the rick-yard, the corn-stack, the cow and bullock yards, the stables, the gardens, and the newly sown or mown fields, in quest of their natural prey, the rat and mouse. In the fields the mice eat and carry off the newly-sown peas or corn, so in the garden, or the ripened garnered corn in stacks; but when the cat is on guard much of this is prevented. Rats eat corn and carry off more, kill whole broods of ducklings and chickens in a night, undermine buildings, stop drains, and unwittingly do much other injury to the well-being of the farmers and others. What a ruinous thing it would be, and what a dreadfully horrible thing it is to be overrun with rats, to say nothing of mice. In this matter man's best friend is the cat. Silent, careful, cautious, and sure, it is at work, while the owner sleeps, with an industry, a will, and purpose that never rests nor tires from dewy eve till rosy morn, when it will glide through "the cat hole" into the barn for repose among the straw, and when night comes, forth again; its usefulness scarcely imagined, much less known and appreciated.

They who remember old Fleet Prison, in Farringdon Street, will scarcely believe that the debtors there confined were at times so neglected as to be absolutely starving; so much so, that a Mr. Morgan, a surgeon of Liverpool, being put into that prison, was ultimately reduced so low by poverty, neglect, and hunger, as to catch mice by the means of a cat for his sustenance. This is stated to be the fact in a book written by Moses Pitt, "The Cries of the Oppressed," 1691.

GENERAL MANAGEMENT

FEEDING.

Adult cats require less food in proportion than kittens, for two reasons. One is this: a kitten is growing, and therefore extra bone, flesh, skin, hair, and all else has to be provided for; while in the adults, these are more or less acquired, and also they procure for themselves, in various ways in country or suburban localities, much live and other food, and no animal is the better for over or excessive feeding, especially if confined, or its chances of exercise contracted.

I have tried many ways or methods of feeding, biscuits of sorts, liver, lights, horseflesh, bread and milk, rice, fish, and cat mixtures, but have always attained the best results by giving new milk as drink, and raw shin of beef for food, with grass, boiled asparagus stems, cabbage-lettuce, or some other vegetable, either cooked or fresh. Good horseflesh is much liked by the cat, and it thrives well on it. I do not believe in either liver or lights as a flesh or bone maker. Besides the beef, there are the "tit-bits" that the household cat not only usually receives, but looks for or expects.

My dear friend, Mr. John Timbs, in "Things not Generally Known," avers that cats are not so fond of fish as flesh, and that the statement that they are is a fallacy. He says, put both before them and they will take the flesh first, and this I have found to be correct. I should only give fresh fish, as a rule, to a cat when unwell, more as an alternative than food.

As raw meat or other raw food is natural to the cat, it is far the best, with vegetables, for keeping the body, coat, and skin in good condition and health, and the securing of a rich, bright, high colour and quality. On no account try to improve these by either medicinal liquids, pills, or condiments; nothing can be much worse, as reflection will prove. If the cat is healthy, it is at its best, and will keep so by proper food; if unwell, then use such medicines as the disease or complaint it suffers from requires, *and not otherwise.* Many horses and other animals have their constitutions entirely ruined by what are called "coat tonics," which are useless, and only believed in and practised by the thoughtless, gullible, and foolish. Does any one, or will any one take pills, powders, or liquids, for promoting the colour or texture of their hair; would any one be so silly? And yet we are coolly told to give such things to our animals. Granted that in illness medicine is of much service, in health it is harmful, and tends to promote disease where none exists.

SLEEPING PLACES.

I much prefer a round basket filled with oat straw to anything else; some urge that a box is better; my cats have a basket. It is well to sprinkle the straw occasionally with Keating's Powder or flour of sulphur, which is a preventive of insect annoyances, and "Prevention is better than cure."

Never shut cats up in close cupboards for the night, there being little or no ventilation; it is most injurious, pure air being as essential to a cat as to a human being.

Always have a box with dry earth near the cat's sleeping place, unless there is an opening for egress near.

Do not, as a rule, put either collar or ribbon on your cat; though they may thereby be improved in appearance, they are too apt to get entangled or caught by the collar, and often strangulation ensues; besides which, in long-haired cats, it spoils their mane or frill. Of course at shows it is allowable.

All cats, as well as other animals, should have ready access to a pan of clear water, which should be changed every day, and the pan cleaned.

Fresh air, sunlight, and warm sunshine are good, both for cats and their owners.

It is related of Charles James Fox that, walking up St. James's Street from one of the club-houses with the Prince of Wales, he laid a wager that he would see more cats than the Prince in his walk, and that he might take which side of the street he liked. When they reached the top, it was found that Mr. Fox had seen thirteen cats, and the Prince not one. The Royal personage asked for an explanation of this apparent miracle. Mr. Fox said: "Your Royal Highness took, of course, the shady side of the way as most agreeable; I knew the sunny side would be left for me, and *cats always prefer the sunshine.*"

A most essential requisite for the health of the cat is cleanliness. In itself the animal is particularly so, as may be observed by its constant habit of washing, or cleaning its fur many times a day; therefore, a clean basket, clean straw, or clean flannel, to lie on— in fact, everything clean is not only necessary, but is a necessity for its absolute comfort.

Mr. Timbs says: "It is equally erroneous that she is subject to fleas; the small insect, which infests the half-grown kitten, being a totally different animal, exceedingly swift in running, but not salient or leaping like a flea."

In this Mr. Timbs slightly errs. Cats *do* have fleas, but not often, and of a different kind to the ordinary flea; but I have certainly seen them jump.

In dressing the coat of the cat no comb should be used, more especially with the long-haired varieties; but if so, which I do not recommend, great care should be used not to drag the hair so that it comes out, or breaks, otherwise a rough, uneven coat will and must be the result.

Should the hair become clotted, matted, or felted, as is sometimes the case, it ought to be moistened, either with oil or soft-soap, a little water being added, and when the application has well soaked in, it will be found comparatively easy to separate the tangle with the fingers by gently pulling out from the mass a few hairs at a time, after which wash thoroughly, and use a soft, long-haired brush; but this must be done with discretion, so as not to spoil the natural waviness of the hair, or to make it lie in breadths instead of the natural, easy, carelessly-parted flaky appearance, which shows the white or blue cat off to such advantage.

WASHING.

Most cats have a dislike to water, and as a rule, and under ordinary conditions, generally keep themselves clean, more especially the short-haired breeds; but, as is well known, the Angora, Persian, and Russian, if not taken care of, are sure to require washing, the more so to prepare them for exhibition, as there is much gain in the condition in which a cat comes before the judge.

There are many cases of cats taking to the water and swimming to certain points to catch fish, or for other food, on record; yet it is seldom that they take a pleasure in playing about in it. I therefore think it well to mention that I had a half-bred black and white Russian, that would frequently jump into the bath while it was being filled, and sit there until the water rose too high for its safety. Thus cats may be taught to like washing.

If a cat is to be washed, treat it as kindly and gently as is possible, speaking in a soothing tone, and in no way be hasty or sudden in your movements, so as to raise distrust or fear. Let the water be warm but not hot, put the cat in slowly, and when its feet rest on the bottom of the tub, you may commence the washing.

Mr. A. A. Clarke, the well-known cat fancier, says: "I seldom wash my cats, I rather prefer giving them a good clean straw-bed, and attending to their general health and condition, and they will then very seldom require washing. I find that much washing makes the coat harsh and poor, and I also know from experience that it is 'a work of art' to wash a cat properly, and requires an artist in that way to do it. My plan is to prepare some liquid soap, by cutting a piece into shreds, and putting it into cold water, and then boiling it for an hour. I then have two clean tubs got ready, one to wash, the other to rinse in. Have soft water about blood heat, with a very small piece of soda in the washing-tub, into which I place the cat, hind-quarters first, having some one that it knows perfectly well, to hold and talk to the cat while the washing is going on. I begin with the tail, and thoroughly rubbing in the soap with my hands, and getting by degrees over the body and shoulders up to the ears, leaving the head until the cat is rinsed in the other tub, which ought to be half filled with warm soft water, into which I place the cat, and thoroughly rinse out all the soap, when at the same time I wash the head, and I then sit in front of the fire and dry with warm towels; and if it is done well and thoroughly, it is a good three hours' hard work."

I would add to the foregoing that I should use Naldire's dog soap, which I have found excellent in all ways, and it also destroys any insect life that may be present.

Also in washing, be careful not to move the hands in circles, or the hair will become entangled and knotty, and very difficult to untwist or unravel. Take the hair in the hands, and press the softened soap through and through the interstices, and when rinsing do the same with the water, using a large sponge for the purpose. After drying I should put the cat in a box lightly, full of oat straw, and place it in front of, or near a fire, at such distance as not to become too warm, and only near enough to prevent a chill before the cat is thoroughly dry.

MATING.

Yet nature is made better by no mean,
But nature makes that mean: so, o'er that art,
Which, you say, adds to nature, is an art
That nature makes.

Coriolanus, Act II. Scene I.

This requires much and careful consideration, and in this, as well as in many other things, experience and theory join hands, while the knowledge of the naturalist and fancier is of great and superlative value; yet, with all combined, anything like certainty can never be assured, although the possession of pedigree is added, and the different properties of food, health, quality, and breed understood and taken into account. Still, much may be gained by continued observation and close study of the peculiar properties of colour, besides that of form. If, for instance, a really, absolutely *blue* cat, without a shade of any other colour, were obtainable, and likewise a pure, clear, canary yellow, there is little doubt that at a distant period, a green would be the ultimate goal of success. But the yellow tabby is not a yellow, nor the blue a blue. There being, then, only a certain variety of colours in cats, the tints to be gained are limited entirely to a certain set of such colours, and the numerous shades and half-shades of these mixed, broken, or not, into tints, markings light or dark, as desired. To all colour arrangements, if I may so call them, by the mind, intellect, or hand of man, there is a limit, beyond which none can go. It is thus far and no further.

There is the black cat, and the white; and between these are intervening shades, from very light, or white-gray, to darker, blue, dark blue, blackish blue, gray and black. If a blue-black is used, the lighter colours are of one tint; if a brown-black, they are another.

127

Then in what are termed the sandies and browns, it commences with the yellow-white tint scarcely visible apart from white to the uninitiated eye; then darker and darker, until it culminates in deep brown, with the intervening yellows, reds, chestnuts, mahoganys, and such colours, which generally are striped with a darker colour of nearly their own shade, until growing denser, it ends in brown-black.

The gray tabby has a ground colour of gray. In this there are the various shades from little or no markings, leaving the colour a brown or gray, or the gray gradually disappearing before the advance of the black in broader and broader bands, until the first is excluded and black is the result.

The tortoiseshell is a mixture of colours in patches, and is certainly an exhibition of what may be done by careful selection, mating, and crossing of an animal while under the control of man, in a state of thorough domestication. What the almond tumbler is to the pigeon fancier, so is the tortoiseshell cat to the cat fancier, or the bizarre tulip to the florist. As regards colour, it is a triumph of art over nature, by the means of skilful, careful mating, continued with unwearying patience. We get the same combination of colour in the guinea-pig, both male and female, and therefore this is in part a proof that by proper mating, eventually a tortoiseshell male cat should soon be by no means a rarity. There are rules, which, if strictly followed under favourable conditions, ought to produce certain properties, such properties that may be desired, either by foolish (which generally it is) fashion, or the production of absolute beauty of form, markings in colours, or other brilliant effects, and which the true fanciers endeavour to obtain. It is to this latter I shall address my remarks, rather than to the reproduction of the curious, the inelegant, or the deformed, such as an undesirable number of toes, which are impediments to utility.

In the first place, the fancier must thoroughly make up his mind as to the variety of form, colour, association of colours or markings by which he wishes to produce, if possible, perfection;

and, having done so, he must provide himself with such stock as, on being mated, are likely to bring such progeny as will enable him in due time to attain the end he has in view. This being gained, he must also prepare himself for many disappointments, which are the more likely to accrue from the reason that, in all probability, he starts without any knowledge of the ancestry or pedigree of the animals with which he begins his operations. Therefore, for this reason, he has to gain his knowledge of any aptitude for divergence from the ordinary or the common they may exhibit, or which his practical experience discovers, and thus, as it were, build up a family with certain points and qualities before he can actually embark in the real business of accurately matching and crossing so as to produce the results which, by a will, undeviating perseverance, and patience, he is hoping to gain eventually—the perfection he so long, ardently, and anxiously seeks to acquire; but he must bear in mind that that, on which he sets his mark, though high, must come within the limits and compass of that which *is* attainable, for it is not the slightest use to attempt that which is not within the charmed circle of possibilities.

TORTOISESHELLS.

I place these first on the list because, being an old pigeon fancier and somewhat of a florist, I deem these to be the breed wherein there is the most art and skill required to produce properly all the varied mottled beauty of bright colours that a cat of this breed should possess; and those who have bred tortoiseshells well know how difficult a task it is.

In breeding for this splendid, gorgeous, and diversified arrangement of colouring, a black, or even a blue, may be used with a yellow or red tabby female, or a white male, supposing either or both were the offspring of a tortoiseshellmother. The same males might be used with advantage with a tortoiseshell female. This is on the theory of whole colours, and patches or portions of whole colours, without bars or markings when possible. In the same way some of the best almond tumbler pigeons are bred from an almond cock mated to a yellow hen. The difficulty here, until lately, has been to breed hens of the varied mottling on almond colour, the hen almost invariably coming nearly, if not quite yellow—so much so that forty to fifty years ago a yellow hen was considered as a pair to an almond cock, in the same way as the red tabby male is now regarded in respect to the tortoiseshell female; and it was not until at Birmingham, many years ago, when acting as judge, I refused to award prizes to them as such, that the effort was made, and a successful one, to breed almond-coloured hens with the same plumage as the cock—that is, the three colours. With cats the matter is entirely different, it being the male at present that is the difficulty, if a real difficulty it may be called.

Mr. Herbert Young, a most excellent cat fancier and authority on the subject, is of opinion that if a tortoiseshell male cat could be found, it would not prove fertile with a tortoiseshell female. But of this I am very doubtful, because, if the red and the yellow tabby is so, which is decidedly a weaker colour, I do not see how it can possess more vitality than a cat marked with the *three* colours; in fact the latter ought, in reality, to be more prolific, having black as one of the colours, which is a strong colour, blue being only the weak substitute, or with white *combined*. A whole black is one of the strongest colours and most powerful of cats.

Reverting once again to the pigeon fancier by way of analogy, take, as an instance, what is termed the silver-coloured pigeon, or the yellow. These two, and duns, are, by loss of certain pigments, differently coloured and constituted (like the tortoiseshell among cats) from other varieties of pigeons of harder colours, such as blues, and blacks, or even reds. For a long time silver turbit cock pigeons were so scarce that, until I bred some myself, I had never seen such a thing; yet hens were common enough, and got from silver and blues. In the nestling before the feathers come, the young of these colours are without down, and are thus thought to be, and doubtless are, a weakly breed; yet there is no absolute diminution of strength, beyond that of colour, when silver is matched to silver; but dun with dun, these last go lower in the scale, losing the black tint, and not unfrequently the colour is yellow; or, matched with black, breed true blacks. I am, therefore, of opinion that a tortoiseshell male and female would, and should, produce the best of tortoiseshells, both male and female.

It not unfrequently happens that from a tortoiseshell mother, in the litter of kittens there are male blacks and clear whites, and I have known of one case when a good blue and one where the mixed colours were blue, light red, and light yellow were produced, while the sisters in the litter were of the usual pure tortoiseshell markings. In such cases, generally, the latter only are kept, unless it is the blue, the others being too often destroyed. My own plan would be to breed from such black or white males, and if not successful in the first attempt, to breed again in the same way with the young obtained with such cross; and I have but little doubt that, by so doing, the result so long sought after would be achieved. At least, I deem it far more likely to be so than the present plan of using the red tabby as the male, which are easily produced, though very few are of high excellence in richness of ground tints.

TORTOISESHELL-AND-WHITE.

If tortoiseshell-and-white are desired, then a black-and-white male may be selected, being bred in the same way as those recommended for the pure tortoiseshell, or one without white if the female has white; but on *no account* should an ordinary tabby be tolerated, but a red tabby female of deep colour, or having white, may be held in request, though I would prefer patches of colour not in any way barred. The gray tabby will throw barred, spotted, or banded kittens, mixed with tortoiseshell, which is the very worst form of mottling, and is very difficult to eradicate. A gray "ticking" will most likely appear between the dark colour, as it does between the black bars of the tabby.

BLACK.

The best black, undoubtedly, are those bred from tortoiseshell mothers or females. The black is generally more dense, and less liable to show any signs of spots, bands, or bars, when the animal is in the sun or a bright light; when this is so, it is fatal to a black as regards its chance of a prize, or even notice, and it comes under the denomination of a black tabby.

If a black and a white cat are mated, let the black be the male, blacks having more stamina, the issue will probably be either white or black; and also when you wish the black to be perpetuated, the black male must be younger. In 1884, a black female cat was exhibited with five white kittens. I have just seen a beautiful black Persian whose mother was a clear white; this, and the foregoing example, prove either colour represents the same for the purpose of breeding to colour.

For breeding black with white, take care that the white is the gray-white, and not the yellow-white; the first generally has orange or yellow eyes, and this is one of the required qualities in the black cat. If a yellow-white with blue eyes, this type of eye would be detrimental, and most likely the eyes of the offspring would have a green stain, or possibly be of odd colours.

It should be borne in mind, that black kittens are seldom or ever so rich in colour when newly born, as they afterwards become; therefore, if without spots or bars, and of a deep self brown-black, they will in all possibility be fine in colour when they gain their adult coat. This the experienced fancier well knows, though the tyro often destroys that which will ultimately prove of value, simply from ignorance. An instance of the brown-black kitten is before me as I write, in a beautiful Persian, which is now changing from the dull kitten self brown-black on to a brilliant glossy, jetty beauty.

BLUES.

Blue in cats is one of the most extraordinary colours of any, for the reason that it is the *mixture* of black which is no colour, and white which is no colour, and this is the more curious because black mated with white generally produces either one colour or the other, or breaks black and white, or white and black. The blue being, as it were, a weakened black, or a withdrawal by white of some, if not all, of the brown or red, varying in tint according to the colour of the black from which it was bred, dark-gray, or from weakness in the stamina of the litter. In the human species an alliance of the Negro, or African race, and the European, produces the mulatto, and some other shades of coloured skin, though the hair generally retains the black hue; but seldom or ever are the colours broken up as in animal life, the only instance that has come to my knowledge, and I believe on record, being that of the spotted Negro boy, exhibited at fairs in England by Richardson, the famous showman; but in this case both the parents were black, and natives of South Africa. The boy arrived in England in September, 1809, and died February, 1813. His skin and hair were everywhere parti-coloured, transparent brown and white; on the crown of his head several triangles, one within the other, were formed by alternations of the colour of the hair.

In other domestic animals blue colour is not uncommon. Blue-tinted dogs, rabbits, horses of a blue-gray, or spotted with blue on a pink flesh colour, as in the naked horse shown at the Crystal Palace some years ago, also pigs; and all these have likewise broken colours of blue, or black, and white. I do not remember having seen any blue cattle, nor any blue guinea-pigs, but no doubt these latter will soon exist. When once the colour or break from the black is acquired, it is then easy to go on multiplying the different shades and varieties of tint and tone, from the dark blue-black to the very light, almost white-gray. In some places in Russia, I am told, blue cats are exceedingly common; I have seen several shown under the names of Archangel, and others as Chartreuse and Maltese cats. Persians are imported sometimes of this colour, both dark and light. Next kin to it is the very light-gray tabby, with almost the same hue, if not quite so light-gray markings. Two such mated have been known to produce very light self grays, and of a lovely hue, a sort of "morning gray"; these matched with black should breed blues. Old male black, and young female white cats, have been known to produce kittens this colour. There is a colony of farm cats at Rodmell, Sussex, from which very fine blues are bred. Light silver tabby males, and white females, are also apt to have one or so in a litter of kittens; but these generally are not such good blues, the colour being a gray-white, or nearly so, should the hair or coat be parted or divided, the skin being light. The very dark, if from brown-black, are not so blue, but come under the denomination of "smokies," or blue "smokies," with scarcely a tint of blue in them; some "smokies" are white, or nearly so, with dark tips to the hair; these more often occur among Persian than English cats, though I once had a smoky tabby bred from a black and a silver tabby. Importations of some of the former are often extremely light, scarcely showing any markings. These, and such as these, are very valuable where a self blue is desired. If these light colours are females, a smoke-coloured male is an excellent cross, as it already shows a weakened colour. For a very light, tender, delicate, light-gray long-haired self, I should try a white male, and either a rich blue, or a soft gray, extremely lightly-marked tabby.

As a rule, all broken whites, such as black and white, should be avoided; because, as I explained at the commencement of these notes on blues, the blue is black and white *amalgamated*, or the brown withdrawn from the colouring, or, if not, with the colours breaking, or becoming black and white. If whole coloured blues are in request, then parti-colours, such as white and black, or black and white, are best excluded. Blue and white are easily attainable by mating a blue male with a white and black female.

The best and deepest coloured of the blue short-haired cats are from Archangel. Those I have seen were very fine in colour, the pelage being the same colour to the skin, which was also dark and of a uniform lilac-tinted blue. Some come by chance. I knew of a blue English cat, winner of several prizes, whose parents were a black and white male mated with a "light-gray tabby" and white; but this was an exception to the rule, for strongly-marked tabbies are not a good cross.

BROWN TABBY.

For the purpose of breeding rich brown black-striped tabbies, a male of a rich dark rufous or red tabby should be selected, the bands being regular and not too broad, the lighter or ground colour showing well between the lines; if the black lines are very broad, it is then a black, striped with brown, instead of a brown with black, which is wrong. With this match a female of a good brown ground colour, marked with dense, not broad, black bands, having clear, sharply defined edges. Note also that the centre line of the back is a distinct line, with the brown ground colour on which it is placed being in no way interspersed with black, and at least as broad as the black line; by this cross finely-marked kittens of a brilliant colour may be expected. But if the progeny are not so bright as required, and the ground colour not glowing enough, then, when the young arrive at maturity, mate with a dark-yellow red tabby either male or female.

Very beautiful brown tabbies are also to be found among the litters of the female tortoiseshell, allied with a dark-brown tabby with narrow black bars. It is a cross that may be tried with advantage for both variety and richness of colour, among which it will not be found difficult to find something worthy of notice.

WHITE.

Of English, or short-haired cats, the best white are those from a tortoiseshell mother, and as often some of the best blacks. These whites are generally of soft yellow, or sandy tint of white. Although they have pink noses, as also are the cushions of their feet, they are not Albinos, not having the peculiar pink or red eyes, nor are they deficient in sight. I have seen and examined with much care some hundreds of white cats, but have never yet seen one with pink eyes, though it has been asserted that such exist, and there is no reason why they should not. Still, I am inclined to think they do not, and the pale blue eyes, or the red tinted blue, like those of the Siamese, take the place of it in the feline race; neither have I ever seen a white horse with pink eyes, but I find it mentioned in one of the daily papers that among other presents to the Emperor of Russia, the Bokhara Embassy took with them ten thoroughbred saddle-horses of different breeds, one of them being a magnificent animal—a pure white stallion with *blue eyes.*

The cold gray-white is the opposite of the black, and this knowledge should not be lost sight of in mating. It generally has yellow or light orange eyes. This colour, in a male, may be crossed with the yellow-white with advantage, when more strength of constitution is required; but otherwise I deem the best matching is that of two yellow-white, both with blue eyes, for soft hair, elegance, and beauty; but even a black male and a white female produce whites, and sometimes blacks, but the former are generally of a coarse description, and harsh in coat by comparison. I think the blue-eyed white are a distinct breed from the common ordinary white cat, nor do I remember any such being bred from those with eyes of yellow colour.

ABYSSINIAN.

To breed these true, it is well to procure imported or pedigree stock, for many cats are bred in England from ordinary tabbies, that so nearly resemble Abyssinian in colour as scarcely to be distinguished from the much-prized foreigners. The males are generally of a darker colour than the females, and are mostly marked with dark-brown bands on the forehead, a black band along the back which ends at the tip of the tail, with which it is annulated. The ticking should be of the truest kind, each hair being of three distinct colours, blue, yellow, or red, and black at the points, the cushions of the feet black, and back of the hind-legs. Choose a female, with either more red or yellow, the markings being the same, and, with care in the selection, there will be some very brilliant specimens. Eyes bright orange-yellow.

ABYSSINIAN CROSSES.

Curiously coloured as the Abyssinian cat is, and being a true breed, no doubt of long far back ancestry, it is most useful in crossing with other varieties, even with the Persian, Russian, Angora, or the Archangel, the ticking hues being easy of transmission, and is then capable of charming and delightful tints, with breadths of beautiful mottled or grizzled colouring, if judiciously mated. The light tabby Persian, matched with a female Abyssinian, would give unexpected surprises, so with the dark blue Archangel; a well-ticked blue would not only be a novelty, but an elegant colour hitherto unseen. A deep red tabby might result in a whole colour, bright red, or a yellow tint. I have seen a cat nearly blackticked with white, which had yellow eyes. It was truly a splendid and very beautiful animal, of a most recherché colour. Matched with a silver-gray tabby, a silver-gray tick is generally the sequence. A yellow-white will possibly prove excellent. Try it!

WHITE AND BLACK.

For white and black choose evenly marked animals, in which white predominates. I have seen three differently bred cats, white, with black ears and tails, all else being white, and been informed of others. I failed to notice the colour of the eyes which came under my own observation, for which I am sorry, for much depends on the colour of the eyes in selection; for though the parents are white and black, many gray and white, tabby and white, even yellow and white will appear among the kittens, gray being the original colour, and black the sport.

BLACK AND WHITE.

A deep brown, dense black ground, with a blaze up the face, white nose and lips, should be chosen—white chest and white feet. Get a female as nearly as possible so marked, and being a dense blue-black, both with orange eyes, when satisfactorily marked, and sable and white kittens may be expected.

BLUE TABBY.

A slate colour, or a blue male cat, mated with a strongly black-marked, though narrow-banded blue or gray tabby, is the best for dark blue tabbies, or a light-gray, evenly-marked female may be used. What a lovely thing a white cat, marked with black stripes, would be! It may be got.

SPOTTED TABBY.

For spotted tabby the best brown are those got by mating a spotted red tabby, the darker the better, and a brown and black spotted female. These should be carefully selected, not only for their ground colour, but also for the roundness, distinctness, blackness, and arrangements of their spots.

For grays, blues, and light ash-coloured tabbies, the same care should be exercised, the only difference being the choice of ground colours.

FANCY COLOURS.

By other odd and fanciful combinations, many beautiful mottles and stripes may be secured, and strange, quaint, harmonious arrangements of lines and spots produced according to "fancy's dictates;" but the foregoing are the chief colours in request for exhibition purposes, and most of the colour marking. In any other colour classes, the beauties, whatever they may be, are chiefly the result of accident or sports, selected for such beauty, or in other ways equally interesting.

CAT AND KITTENS

Care and attention is necessary when the cat is likely to become a mother. A basket or box, half filled with sweet hay, or clean oat straw, with some flannel in the winter, is absolutely requisite, and a quiet nook or corner selected away from light, noise, and intrusion. Some prefer a box made like a rabbit-hutch, with sleeping place, and a barred door to one or both compartments which may be closed when thought necessary for comfort and quiet. The cat should be placed within, with food and new milk by or inside, and there be regularly fed for a few days, all pans and plates to be kept well washed, and only as much food given at a time as can be eaten at one meal, so that everything is clean and fresh. Cats, as I have before stated, delight in cleanliness, therefore this, nor any comfort, should not be forgotten or omitted, for so much depends on her health and the growth of her little family, with regard to their future well-being.

The cat brings forth three times a year, and often more. The time of gestation is to sixty-three days, and the number of the kittens varies much. Some will have five to six at a birth, while others *never* have more than two or three. I had a blue tabby, "The Old Lady," which never had more than *one*. The cat, however, is a very prolific animal, and, if of long life, produces a very numerous progeny. *The Derby Gazette*, December 10th, 1886, states:—"There is a cat at Cromford, the age of which is nineteen years. It belonged to the late Mr. Isaac Orme, who died a few months ago. The old man made an entry of all the kittens the cat had given birth to, which, up to the time of his death, numbered 120. It has now just given birth to *one* more. It will not leave the house where the old man died, except to visit a neighbouring house, where there is a harmonium; and when the instrument is being played, the cat will go and stand on its hind-legs beside the player."

Cats live to various ages, the oldest I have seen being twenty-one years, and the foregoing is the greatest age at which I have known one to breed. But I am indebted to Mrs. Paterson, of Tunbridge Wells, for the information that Mr. Sandal had a cat that lived to the extraordinary age of twenty-four years. I have seen Mr. Sandal, and found that such was the case. It was a short-haired cat, and rather above the usual size, and tabby in colour.

When littered, the kittens are weak, blind, deaf, helpless little things, and it appears almost impossible they can ever attain the supple grace and elegance of form and motion so much admired in the fully-developed cat.

The state of visual darkness continues until the eighth or ninth day, during which the eyesight is gradually developing. After this they grow rapidly, and, at the age of a few weeks, the gamboling, frolicsome life of "kittenhood" begins, and they begin to feed, lap milk, if slightly warm, when placed in front of them.

No animal is more fond and attentive than the cat; she is the most tender and gentle of nurses, watching closely every movement of her young. With the utmost solicitude she brings the choicest morsels of her own food, which she lays before them, softly purring, while with gentle and motherly ways she attracts them to the spot while she sits or stands, looking on with evident satisfaction, full of almost uncontrollable pleasure and delight, at their eager, but often futile attempts and endeavours to eat and enjoy the dainty morsel. Yet nothing is wasted, for after waiting what appears to her a reasonable time, and giving them every encouragement, and with the most exemplary patience, she teaches them what they should do, and how, by slowly making a meal of the residue herself, frequently stopping and fondling and licking them in the hope they will yet make another effort. What can be more sensitively touching than the following anecdote, sent to *The Animal World* by C. E. N., in 1876? It is a little poem of everyday life, full of deep feeling and feline love.

"I have a small tabby cat, very comely and graceful. Being very fond of her kitten, she is always uneasy if she loses sight of it if only for a short time. For the last six weeks, the mother, failing to recall the truant back by her voice, even returns to the kitchen for the lower portion of a rabbit's fore-leg, which has served as a plaything for some time. With this in her mouth, she proceeds to search for her lost one, crying all the time, and, putting it down at her feet, repeats her entreaties, to which the kitten, allured by the sight of its plaything, generally responds. Owing to its gambols in the open air during the inclement weather, the kitten was seized with an affliction of the throat; the mother, puzzled with the prostration of its offspring, brought down the rabbit's foot to attract attention. In vain; the kitten died. Even now the loving mother searches for the rabbit's foot, and brings it down."

An instance of the peculiar foresight and instinct, so often observable in the cat, is related in *The Animal World*, October, 1882. Miss M. writes: "This house is very old, and big impudent rats often appear in the shop, so a cat is always kept on the premises. Pussy is about five years old, and is a handsome, light tortoiseshell, with a pretty face and coaxing ways. A month ago she had three kittens, one of which was kept; they were born in the drawing-room, by the side of the piano. When the two were taken away, pussy carried the one remaining to the fireplace, and made it a bed under the grate with shavings. When a fortnight old, both were removed downstairs to the room behind the shop. One day last week an enormous rat appeared; pussy spied him, and set up her back; but her motherly instinct prevailed. She looked round the shop, and, finding a drawer high up a little way open, she jumped with her kitten in her mouth, and dropped it into the drawer, after which she descended and fought a battle royal with the rat, which she soon despatched and carried to her mistress, then went back to the drawer and brought out her kitten."

Here is another fact as regards the observation of cats, which possibly, in this respect, is not far different from some other domestic animals. "A gray and white cat, 'Jenny' (a house cat), had three kittens in the hollow stump of an old ash-tree, some distance from the house. There, from time to time, she took them food, and there nursed them. One day, looking from the window, I observed a very heavy storm was approaching, and also, what should I see but Mistress 'Jenny' running across the meadow as fast as she could, and, on her drawing nearer, I noticed that she had one of her kittens in her mouth. She ran past and put the kitten into a small outhouse, when she immediately hastened back, and returned bringing another of her kittens, which she put in the same place. Again she started for the wood, and shortly reappeared bringing her third and last kitten, though more slowly, seemingly very tired. I was just thinking of going to help her, when she suddenly quickened her pace and ran for the outhouse; just then a few drops of rain began to fall. In a few moments a deluge of water was falling, the lightning was flashing, the thunder crashed overhead and rumbled in the distance, but 'Jenny' did not mind, for she had her three kittens comfortably housed, and she and they were all nestled together in an apple basket, warm and dry. Surely she must have known, by instinct or observation, that the storm was coming."—From my Book of "*Animal Stories, Old and New.*"

Should it be deemed necessary to destroy some, if not all of the litter, which, unfortunately, is sometimes the case, it is not well to take away the whole at once; but it is advisable to let a day or two intervene between each removal; the mother will thus be relieved of much suffering, especially if one at least is left for her to rear, but two is preferable. Still, when the progeny are well-marked or otherwise valuable, and large specimens are required for show or other purposes, three kittens are enough to leave, though some advocate as many as five; but if this is done it is better to provide a foster-mother for two, for which even a dog will often prove a very good substitute for one of the feline race. In either case, slightly warm new milk should be given at least three times a day; the milk should not be heated, but some hot water put to it, and as soon as their teeth are sufficiently grown for them to be of use in mastication give some raw beef cut very small and fine. Some prefer chopped liver; I do not; but never give more than they can lap or eat at each meal. This liberal treatment will make a wonderful difference in their growth, and also their general health and strength; and being so fed makes them more docile. And it should be borne in mind that in a state of nature cats always bring raw food to their young as soon as they are able to eat; therefore raw meat is far the best to give them—their dentition proves this.

KITTENS

Kittenhood, the baby time especially of country cats, is with most the brightest, sprightliest, and prettiest period of their existence, and perhaps the most happy. True, when first born and in the earliest era of their lives, they are blind, helpless little things, dull, weak, and staggering, scarcely able to stand, if at all, almost rolling over at every attempt, making querulous, fretful noises, if wakeful or cold, or for the time motherless. But 'tis not for long; awhile, and she, the fondest of mothers, is with them. They are nestled about her, or amid her soft, warm fluffy fur, cossetted with parental tenderness, caressed, nurtured, and, with low, sweet tones and fondlings, they are soothed again and again to sleep.—They sleep.—Noiseless, and with many a longing, lingering look, the careful, watchful, loving creature slowly and reluctantly steals away; soon to return, when she and her little ones are lost "in the land of dreams." And so from day to day, until bright, meek-eyed, innocent, inquiring little faces, with eager eyes, peep above the basket that is yet their home. One bolder than the others springs out, when, scared at its own audacity, as quickly, and oft clumsily, scrambles back, then out— in—and out, in happy, varied, wild, frolicsome, gambolsome play, they clutch, twist, turn, and wrestle in artless mimicry of desperate quarrelling;—the struggle over, in liveliest antics they chase and rechase in turn, or in fantastic mood play; 'tis but play, and such wondrous play—bright, joyous, and light; and so life glides on with them as kittens—frisky, skittish, playful kittens.

A few more days, and their mother leads them forth, with many an anxious look and turn, softly calling in a subdued voice, they halting almost at every step; suddenly, oft at nothing, panic-stricken, quickly scamper back, not one yet daring to follow where all is so oddly strange and new, their natural shyness being stronger than the love of freedom. Again, with scared look and timid steps, they come, when again at nothing frightened, or with infantile pretence, they are off, "helter-skelter," without a pause or stay, one and all, they o'er and into their basket clamber, tumble in, turn about and stare with a more than half-bewildered, self-satisfied safety look about them. Gaining courage once more, they peer about, with dreamy, startled, anxious eyes, watching for dangers that never are, although expected. Noiseless comes their patient, loving mother; with what new delight they cling about her; how fondly and tenderly she tends them, lures, cossets, coaxes, and talks, as only a gentle mother-cat can—"There is no danger, no!—nothing to fear. Is she not with them; will she not guard, keep and defend them? There is a paradise out there; through this door; they must see it. Come, she will show them; come, have confidence! Now, then—come!" When followed by her three little ones, and they with much misgiving, she passes out—out into the garden, out among the lovely, blooming, fragrant roses, out among the sweet stocks and the damask-coloured gilly-flowers, the pink daisies, brown, red, and orange wallflowers, the spice-scented pinks, and other gay and modest floral beauties that make so sweet the soft and balmy breath of Spring. Out into the sunshine, almost dazed amid a flood of light, warmed by the glowing midday sun. Light above, light around and everywhere about; while the sweet-scented breezes come joy-laden with the happy wild birds' melodious songs; wearied with wonderment, under the flower-crowned lilacs they gather themselves to rest. How beautiful all is, how full of young delights; the odorous wind fans, soothes, and lulls them to rest, while rustling leaves softly whisper them to sleep—they and their loving mother slumber unconscious of all things, and with all things at peace. There, stretched in the warm sunshine asleep, possibly dreaming of their after-life when they are kittens no longer, they rest and—sleep.

Their young, bright life has begun; how charming all is, how peaceful under the young, green leaves, bright as emeralds; about them flickering, chequering lights play with the never-wearying, restless shadows; they know of nothing but bliss, so happy, they enjoy all—sweet-faced, gentle-eyed and pretty. Happy, there is no other word. "Happy as a kitten." "Sprightly as a kitten." As they sleep they dream of delight, awake they more than realise their dreams.

OF KITTENS IN GENERAL

Kittens usually shed their first teeth from five to seven months old, and seldom possess even part of a set of the small, sharp dentition after that time. When shown as kittens under six months old, and they have changed the *whole* of their kittenhood teeth for those of the adult, it is generally considered a fairly *strong* proof that their life is in excess of that age, and the judge is therefore certainly justified in disqualifying such exhibit, though sometimes, as in other domestic animals, there occurs premature change, as well as inexplicable delay.

Kittens are not so cleanly in their habits as cats of a mature growth; this is more generally the case when they have been *separated from the mother-cat*, or when removed to some place that is strange to them, or when sufficient care is not taken, by letting them out of the house occasionally. When they cannot from various reasons be so turned out, a box should be provided, partly filled with dry earth, to which they may retire. This is always a requisite when cats or kittens are valuable, and therefore obliged to be kept within doors, especially in neighbourhoods where there is a chance of their being lost or stolen.

It should also be borne in mind, that the present and future health of an animal, be it what it may, is subject to many incidences, and not the least of these is good and appropriate food, shelter, warmth, and cleanliness. It is best to feed at regular intervals. In confinement, Mr. Bartlett, the skilful and experienced manager of the Zoological Society's Gardens, at Regent's Park, finds that one meal a day is sufficient, and this is thought also to be the case with a full-grown cat, more especially when it has the opportunity of ranging and getting other food, such as mice, and "such small deer;" but with "young things" it is different, as it is deemed necessary to get as much strength and growth as possible. I therefore advocate several meals a day, at least three, with a variety of food, such as raw shin of beef, cut very small; bones to pick; fish of sorts, with all the bones taken out, or refuse parts; milk, with a little hot water; boiled rice or oatmeal, with milk or without it; and grass, if possible; if not, some boiled vegetables, stalks of asparagus, cabbage, or even carrots. Let the food be varied from time to time, but never omitting the finely-cut raw beef every day. I am not in favour of liver, or "lights," as it is called, either for cats or kittens. If horseflesh can be depended on, it is a very favourite and strengthening food, and may be given. The kitten should be kept warm and dry, and away from draughts.

Also take especial care not in any way to frighten, tease, or worry a young animal, but do everything possible to give confidence and engender regard, fondness, or affection for its owner; always be gentle and yet firm in its training. Do not allow it to do one day uncorrected, that for which it is punished the next for the same kind of fault. If it is doing wrong remove it, speaking gently, *at the time*, and not *wait long after the fault is committed*, or they will not know what the punishment is for. Many animals' tempers are spoiled entirely by this mode of proceeding.

Take care there is always a clean vessel, with pure clear water for them to drink when thirsty.

Miss Moore's kitten, "Chloe."

MANAGEMENT
OF KITTENS AND CATS

These require quiet and kindly treatment. Do nothing quickly or suddenly, so as in any way to scare or frighten, but when speaking to them, let the voice be moderated, gentle, and soft in tone. Cats are not slow to understand kind treatment, and may often be seen to watch the countenance as though trying to fathom our thoughts. Some cats are of a very timorous nature, and are thus easily dismayed. Others again are more bold in their ways and habits, and are ever ready for cossetty attention; but treat both as you would be treated—kindly.

As to food, as already noted, I have found raw beef the best, with milk mixed with a little hot water to drink—never boil it—and give plenty of grass, or some boiled vegetable, such as asparagus, sea-kale, or celery; they also are fond of certain weeds, such as cat-mint, and equisetum, or mares' or cats' tails, as it is sometimes called. If fish is given it is best mixed with either rice or oatmeal, and boiled, otherwise it is apt to produce diarrhœa.

Horse-flesh may be given as a change, provided that it is not from a diseased animal; and should be boiled, and be fresh.

Brown bread and milk is also good and healthy food; the bread should be cut in cubes of half an inch, and the warm milk and water poured on; only enough for one meal should be prepared at a time.

Let the cat and kittens have as much fresh air as is possible; and if fed on some dainty last thing at night they will be sure to "come in," and thus preserved from doing and receiving injury.

If cats are in any way soiled in their coat, especially the long-haired varieties, and cannot cleanse themselves, they may be washed in warm, soapy water; but this is not advisable in kittens, unless great care is used to prevent their taking cold.

Some cats like being brushed, and it is often an improvement to the pelage or fur if carefully done; but in all cases the brush should have soft, close hair, which should be rather long than otherwise.

Do not let your cats or kittens wear collars or ribbons always, especially if they are ramblers, for the reason that they are liable to get caught on spikes of railings or twigs of bushes, and so starved to death, or strangled, unless discovered.

For sending cats to an exhibition, a close-made basket is best, which will allow for ventilation, as fresh air is most essential; and have it sufficiently large to allow of the cat standing and turning about, especially if a long journey is before them. I have *seen* cats sent to shows taken out of *small boxes*, *dead*, stifled to death—"poor things."

Bear in mind that the higher and better condition your cat is in on its arrival at the show, the greater is the chance of winning.

Do not put carpet or woollen fabrics in the basket, but plenty of good, sweet hay or oat-straw; this will answer all purposes, and does not get sodden.

If you use a padlock for the fastening, *do not forget to send the key to the manager of the show*, as is sometimes the case.

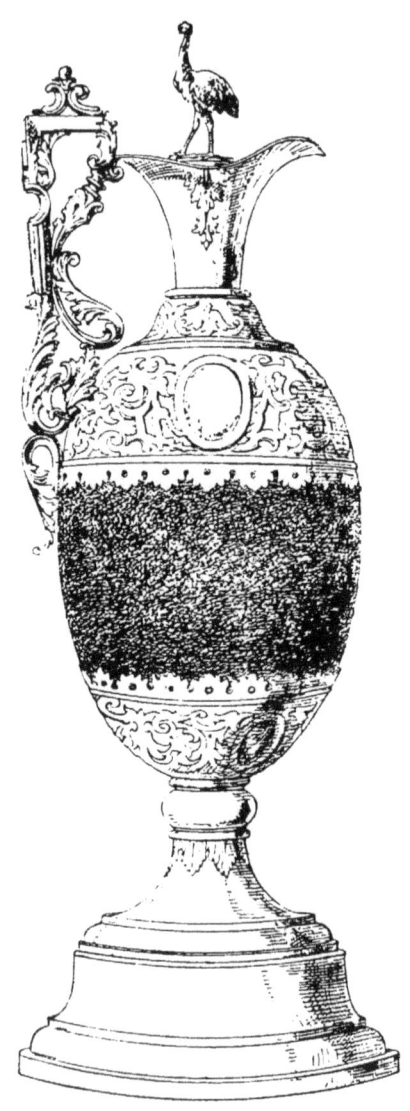

Cat Club Challenge Cup.

POINTS BY WHICH CATS ARE JUDGED

AS SPECIFIED BY MYSELF.

(Revised and corrected to the present time.)

.....What you do,
Still betters what is done.

Winter's Tale, Act IV.

155

THE TORTOISESHELL.

	Points
Head	15
Small, broad across and between the eyes, rounded above, below tapering towards the lips, nose rather long than short, ears of medium size, narrow and rounded at the apex, broad at the base.	
Eyes	10
Orange-yellow, clear, brilliant, large, full, round, and lustrous.	
Fur	10
Short, of even length, smooth, silky, and glossy.	
Colour	25
A mixture of three colours—black, red, and yellow—each to be distinct and clear of the other, with sharp edges, not one colour running into the other, but in small irregular patches, of great brilliancy of tint, the red and yellow to preponderate over the black. If the colours are deep and rich, and the variegation harmonious, the effect is very fine. White is a disqualification.	
Form	15
Narrow, long, graceful in line, neck rather long and slender; shoulders receding, well-sloped and deep; legs medium length, not thick nor clumsy; feet round and small.	
Tail	10
Long, thick at the base, and narrowing towards the end, carried low, with graceful curve, and well-marked with alternate patches of black, red, and yellow.	
Size and Condition	15

Large, lithe, elegant in all its movements; hair smooth, clean, bright, full of lustre, and lying close to the body, all betokening full health and strength.	
Total	100

TORTOISESHELL AND WHITE.

	Points
Head	10
Small, broad across and between the eyes, rounded above, below tapering towards the lips, nose rather long than short, ears medium size, narrow and rounded at the apex, broad at the base.	
Eyes	10
Orange-yellow, clear, brilliant, large, full, round, and lustrous.	
Fur	10
Short, of even length, smooth, silky, and glossy.	
Colour	25
A mixture of three—black, red, and yellow—each to be distinct and clear of the other, with sharp edges, not one colour running into the other, but in small irregular patches of great brilliancy of tint, the red and yellow to preponderate over the black. If the colours are deep and rich, and the variegation harmonious, the effect is very fine.	
White Marking	15
The fore-legs, breast, throat, lips and a circle round them, with a blaze up the forehead, white; lower half of the hind-legs white, nose and cushions of the feet white.	
Form	10

Narrow, long, graceful in line, neck rather long and slender; shoulders receding, well-sloped and deep; legs medium length, not thick nor clumsy; feet round and small.	
Tail	10
Long, thick at the base and narrowing towards the end, carried low, with graceful curve, and well-marked with >alternate patches of black, red, and yellow.	
Size and Condition	10
Large, lithe, elegant in all its movements; hair smooth, clean, bright, full of lustre, and lying close to the body, all betokening full health and strength.	
Total	100

WHITE. SHORT-HAIR.

	Points
Head	15
Small, broad across and between the eyes, rounded above, below tapering towards the lips, nose rather long than short, ears of medium size, narrow and rounded at apex, broad at the base.	
Eyes	15
Blue—a soft, turquoise blue—but yellow is permissible as five points only, green a defect; large, round, and full.	
Fur	15
Short, of even length, smooth, silky, and glossy.	
Colour	15
Yellow-white; gray-white, five points less.	
Form	15

Narrow, long, graceful in line, neck rather long and slender; shoulders receding, well-sloped and deep; legs medium length, not thick nor clumsy; feet round and small.	
Tail	10
Long, thick at the base and narrowing towards the end, carried low, with graceful curve.	
Size and Condition	15
Large, lithe, and elegant in all its movements; hair smooth, clean, bright, full of lustre, and lying close to the body, all betokening good health and strength.	
Total	100

SELF-COLOUR, BLACK, BLUE, GRAY, OR RED SHORT-HAIR.

	Points
Head	15
Small, broad across and between the eyes, rounded above, below tapering towards the lips, nose rather long than short, ears of medium size, narrow, rounded at apex, broad at the base.	
Eyes	15
Orange for black, orange-yellow for blue, deep yellow for gray, and gold tinged with green for red. Large, round, and full; very bright.	
Fur	10
Short, of even length, smooth, silky, and glossy.	
Form	15

159

Narrow, long, graceful in line; neck rather long and slender; shoulders receding, well-sloped and deep; legs medium length, not thick nor clumsy; feet round and small.	
Colour	25
Black, a jet, dense, brown-black, with purple gloss; blue, a bright, rich, even, dark colour, or lighter, but even in tint; gray, a bright, light, even colour; red, a brilliant sandy or yellowish-red colour.	
Tail	5
Long, thick at the base, and narrowing towards the end, carried low, with graceful curve.	
Size and Condition	15
Large, lithe, elegant in all its movements; hair smooth, clean, bright, full of lustre, lying close to the body, all betokening good health and strength.	
Total	100

BROWN AND ORDINARY
TABBY, STRIPED, SHORT-HAIR.

	Points
Head	10
Small, broad across and between the eyes, rounded above, below tapering towards the lips, nose rather long than short, ears of medium size, narrow and rounded at apex, broad at the base.	
Eyes	15
Orange-yellow, slightly tinted with green, large, full, round, and very lustrous.	
Fur	10
Short, of even length, smooth, silky, and glossy.	

Colour	20
Deep, very rich reddish-brown, more rufous inside the legs and belly; ears and nose a still deeper red-brown, the latter at the tip edged with black. Ordinary tabby, dark gray, and ticked.	
Markings	20
Jet-black lines, not too broad, scarcely so wide as the ground colour shown between, so as to give a light and brilliant effect. When the black lines are broader than the colour space, it is a defect, being then black marked with colour, instead of colour marked with black. The lines must be clear, sharp, and well-defined, in every way distinct, having no mixture of the ground colour. Head and legs marked regularly, the rings on the throat and chest being in no way blurred or broken, but clear, graceful, and continuous; lips, cushions of feet, and backs of hind-legs, and the ear-points, black.	
Form	10
Narrow, long, graceful in line, neck rather long and slender; shoulders receding, well-sloped and deep; legs medium length, not thick nor clumsy; feet round and small.	
Tail	5
Long, thick at the base and narrowing towards the end, carried low, with graceful curve, and marked with black rings.	
Size and Condition	10
Large, lithe, elegant in all its movements; hair smooth, clean, bright, full of lustre, and lying close to the body, all betokening full health and strength.	
Total	100

CHOCOLATE, CHESTNUT, RED, OR YELLOW TABBY, STRIPED, SHORT-HAIR.

	Points
Head	10
Small, broad across and between the eyes, rounded above, below tapering towards the lips, nose rather long than short, ears of medium size, narrow and rounded at apex, broad at the base.	
Eyes	15
Orange, gold, or yellow, in the order of the above names, large, round, full, and very lustrous.	
Fur	10
Short, of even length, smooth, silky, and glossy.	
Colour	20
Deep, rich, reddish-brown, bright red, or yellow, in the order as above, brighter inside the legs and belly; ears and nose deeper colour, the latter at the tip red, edged with chocolate.	
Markings	20
Dark, rich brown or chocolate, lines not too broad, scarcely so wide as the ground colour shown between, so as to give a light and brilliant effect; when the lines are broader than the colour space it is a defect, being then light colour markings on dark brown or chocolate, red or dark yellow, instead of colour marked with deeper colour. Head and legs marked regularly, the rings on the throat and chest being in no way blurred or broken, but clear, graceful, and continuous; lips, cushions of feet, and the back of hind-legs, and the ear-points, dark. Yellow tabby, the cushions of feet red, or light red.	
Form	10

Narrow, long, graceful in line, neck rather long and slender, shoulders receding, well-sloped, and deep, legs medium length, not thick nor clumsy, feet round and small.	
Tail	5
Long, thick at the base, and narrowing towards the end, carried low, with graceful curve, and marked with dark rings.	
Size and Condition	10
Large, lithe, elegant in all its movements; hair smooth, clean, bright, full of lustre, and lying close to the body, all betokening full health and strength.	
Total	100

BLUE, SILVER, LIGHT GRAY, AND WHITE TABBY, STRIPED, SHORT-HAIR.

	Points
Head	10
Small, broad across and between the eyes, rounded above, below tapering towards the lips; nose rather long than short; ears of medium size, narrow and rounded at the apex, broad at the base.	
Eyes	15
Orange-yellow for blue tabby; deep, bright yellow for silver or gray; large, full, round, and very lustrous.	
Fur	10
Short, of even length, smooth, silky, and glossy.	
Colour	20
If blue, a rich, deep, yet bright colour; silver, a lighter, yet bright tint; gray, very light; if a white tabby, ground to be colourless; ears and nose a deep gray, the tip red, edged with black.	

Markings	20
Jet-black lines, not too broad, scarcely so wide as the ground colour shown between, so as to give a light and brilliant effect. When the black lines are broader than the colour space, it is a defect, being then black marked with colour, instead of colour with black. The lines must be clear, sharp, and well-defined, in every way distinct, having no mixture of the ground colour. Head and legs marked regularly, the rings on the throat and chest being in no way blurred or broken, but clear, graceful, and continuous; lips, cushions of feet, and the backs of hind-legs, and the ear-points, black.	
Form	10
Narrow, long, graceful in line, neck rather long and slender; shoulders receding, well-sloped, and deep; legs medium length, not thick nor clumsy; feet round and small.	
Tail	5
Long, thick at the base and narrowing towards the end, carried low, with graceful curve, and marked with black rings.	
Size and Condition	10
Large, lithe, elegant in all its movements; hair smooth, clean, bright, full of lustre, and lying close to the body, all betokening full health and strength.	
Total	100

Mr. Babb's Spotted Silver Tabby.

SHORT-HAIRED, SPOTTED TABBIES OF ANY COLOUR.

These to be the same in all points of head, eyes, fur, form, colours, tail, size and condition as those laid down for the judging of short-haired tabby cats in general, with the exception, in whatever colour the markings are, or on whatever ground, they, instead of being in lines or bands, are to be broken up into clear, well-defined and well-formed spots, each spot to be separate, and distinct, and good, firm and dark in colour; these then count as many points as a finely-striped cat in its class.

Properly marked black and white.

BLACK AND WHITE, GRAY-WHITE, RED AND WHITE, AND OTHER COLOURS AND WHITE.

The self colour to count the same number of points as the ground colour in tabby, namely, twenty points, and the white *markings* the same as the tabby markings, that is, twenty points. The other points also the same.

The markings to be: lips, mouth and part of the cheek, including the whiskers, with a blaze up the nose, coming to a point between the eyes, white; throat and chest white, and pear-shaped in outline of colour; all four feet white.

WHITE AND BLACK, WHITE AND GRAY, WHITE AND RED, WHITE AND ANY OTHER COLOUR.

The colours and markings to count the same as the above. The ground colour being white, and markings the dark colour instead of white. In the markings they should be even or well-balanced, such as two black ears, the rest white; or two black ears, with black tail, and the rest white; or all white, with dark tail only. These are not very uncommon markings, but if so marked, they may also have a spot or two on the back or sides provided they balance in size of colour. But the simplicity of the former is the best.

All other fancy colours and markings must be judged according to taste, and entered in the any other variety of colours for short-haired cats, such as strawberry colour, smokies, chinchillas, ticked, black tabbies and such fancy colours.

ABYSSINIAN.

	Points
Head	10
Small, broad across the eyes, rather long than short, nose medium length, all well-formed.	
Eyes	15
Orange-yellow, slightly tinged with green, large, round, full, and bright.	
Nose and Feet	10
Nose dark red, edged with black; tips and cushions of feet black, also the back of the hind-legs.	
Fur	15
Soft, rather woolly hair, yet soft, silky, lustrous, and glossy, short, smooth, even, and dense.	
Ears	10
The usual size of the ordinary English cat, but a little more rounded, with not much hair in the interior, black at the apex.	
Colour	20

A rich, dun brown, ticked with black and orange, or darker on lighter colours, having a dark or black line along the back extending to the end of the tail, and slightly annulated with black or dark colour. As few other marks as possible. Inside of fore-legs and belly to be orange-brown. No white.	
Size and Condition	10
Large; coat glossy and smooth, fitting close to the body; eyes bright and clear.	
Carriage and Appearance	10
Graceful, lithe, elegant, alert and quick in all its movements, head carried up, tail trailing, in walk undulating.	
Total	100

N.B.—The Abyssinian Silver Gray, or Chinchilla, is the same in all points, with the exception of the ground colour being silver instead of brown. This is a new and beautiful variety.

ROYAL CAT OF SIAM.

	Points
Head	10
Small, broad across and between the eyes, tapering upwards and somewhat narrow between the ears: forehead flat and receding, nose long, and somewhat broad, cheeks narrowing towards the mouth, lips full and rounded, ears rather large and wide at base, with very little hair inside.	
Fur	10
Very short, and somewhat woolly, yet soft and silky to the touch, and glossy, with much lustre on the face, legs, and tail.	
Colour	20

168

The ground or body colour to be of an even tint, slightly darker on the back, but not in any way clouded or patched with any darker colour; light rich dun is the preferable colour, but a light fawn, light silver-gray, or light orange is allowable; deeper and richer browns, almost chocolate, are admissible if even and not clouded, but the first is the true type, the last merely a variety of much beauty and excellence; but the dun and light tints take precedence.	
Markings	20
Ears black, the colour not extending beyond them, but ending in a clear and well-defined outline; around the eyes, and all the lower part of the head, black; legs and tail black, the colour not extending into or staining the body, but having a clear line of demarkation.	
Eyes	15
Rather of almond shape, slanting towards the nose, full and of a very beautiful blue opalesque colour, luminous and of a reddish tint in the dusk of evening or by artificial light.	
Tail	5
Short by comparison with the English cat, thin throughout, a little thicker towards the base, without any break or kink.	
Size and Form	10
Rather small, lithe, elegant in outline, and graceful, narrow and somewhat long; legs thin and a little short than otherwise; feet long, not so round as the ordinary cat; neck long and small.	
Condition	10
In full health, not too fat, hair smooth, clear, bright, full of lustre, lying close to the body, which should be hard and firm in the muscles.	
Total	100

MANX, OR SHORT-TAILED CAT.

	Points
Head	10
Small, round, but tapering towards the lips, rather broad across the eyes, nose medium length, ears rather small, broad at base and sloping upwards to a point.	
Eyes	10
According to colour, as shown in other varieties.	
Fur	10
Short, of even length, smooth, silky, and glossy.	
Colour	15
To range the same as other short-haired cats, if self same as self, if marked same as the marked varieties, with less points, allowing for the tail points in this variety.	
Form	15
Narrow, long, neck long and thin, all to be graceful in line; shoulders narrow, well-sloped; fore-legs medium length and thin; hind-legs long in proportion and stouter built; feet round and small.	
Tail	25
To have no tail whatever, not even a stump, but some true bred have a very short, thin, twisted tail, that cannot be straightened, this allowable, and is true bred; but thick stumps, knobs, or short, thick tails *disqualify*.	
Size and Condition	15
Large, elegant in all its movements, hair smooth, clean, bright, full of lustre, and lying close to the body, all betokening good health and strength.	
Total	100

Mr. Clarke's "Miss Whitey."

WHITE, LONG-HAIRED CAT.

	Points
Head	10
Round and broad across and between the eyes, of medium size; nose rather short, pink at the tip; ears ordinary size, but looking small, being surrounded with long hair, which should also be long on the forehead and lips.	
Eyes	15
Large, full, round or almond-shape, lustrous, and of a beautiful azure blue. Yellow admissible as five points only. Green a defect.	
Ruff or Frill	15
Large, very long, flowing, and lion-like, extending over the shoulders, and covering the neck and chest thickly.	
Fur	15

Very long everywhere, mostly along the back, sides, legs, and feet, making tufts between the toes, and points at the apex of the ears.	
Quality of Fur	10
Fine, silky, and very soft in the Persian, with a slightly woolly texture in the Angora, and still more so in the Russian.	
Tail	10
In the Persian the hair long and silky throughout, but somewhat longer at the base. Angora more like the brush of a fox, but much longer in the hair. Russian equally long in hair, but full tail, shorter and more blunt, like a tassel.	
Size, Shape, and Condition	15
Large, small in bone, looking larger than it really is on account of the length of hair. Body long, legs short, tail carried low—not over the back, which is a fault. Fur clean, bright and glossy, even and smooth, and flakey, which gives an appearance of quality.	
Colour	10
White, with a tender, very slightly yellow tint; cushions of feet and tip of nose pink.	
Total	100

BLACK, BLUE, GRAY, RED, OR ANY SELF COLOUR LONG-HAIRED CATS.

	Points
Head	10
Round, and broad across and between the eyes, of medium size; nose rather short and dark at tip, excepting in the red, when it should be pink; ears ordinary size, but looking small, being surrounded with long hair, which should also be long on the forehead and lips.	
Eyes	10
For black, orange; orange-yellow for blue; deep yellow for gray; and gold, tinged with green, for red; large, round, or almond-shaped, full and very bright.	
Ruff or Frill	15
Large, very long, flowing, and lion-like, extending over the shoulders, and covering the neck and chest thickly.	
Fur	15
Very long everywhere; mostly so along the back, sides, legs, and feet, making tufts between the toes, and points at the apex of the ears.	
Quality of Fur	10
Fine, silky, and very soft in the Persian, with slightly woolly texture in the Angora, and still more so in the Russian.	
Tail	10
In the Persian the hair long and silky throughout, but somewhat longer at the base; Angora like the brush of a fox, but longer in the hair; Russian equally long in hair but more full at the end, tail shorter, rather blunt, like a tassel.	
Size, Shape, and Condition	10

173

Large, small in bone, looking larger than it really is on account of the length of the hair; body long, legs short; tail carried low, not over the back, which is a fault; furclean and glossy, even, smooth, and flakey, which gives an appearance of quality.	
Colour	20
Black, dense, bright brown-black, with purple gloss; blue, a bright, rich, even dark colour, or lighter, but even in tint; gray, a bright, light, even colour; red, a brilliant, sandy, or yellowish-red colour.	
Total	100

BROWN, BLUE, SILVER, LIGHT GRAY, AND WHITE TABBY LONG-HAIRED CATS.

	Points
Head	10
Round and broad across and between the eyes, of medium size; nose rather short; ears ordinary size, but looking small, being surrounded with long hair, which should also be long on the forehead and lips.	
Eyes	10
Orange-yellow for brown and blue tabby, very slightly tinted with green; deep, bright yellow for silver; gray, and golden yellow for white tabby; large, full, round, or almond-shaped, and very lustrous.	
Ruff or Frill	10
Large, very long, flowing, and lion-like, extending over the shoulders, and covering the neck and chest thickly.	
Fur	10
Very long everywhere, mostly so along the back, sides, legs, and feet, making tufts between the toes, and points at the apex of the ears.	
Quality of Fur	10
Fine, silky, and very soft in the Persian, with slightly woolly texture in the Angora, and still more so in the Russian.	
Tail	10
In the Persian the hair long and silky throughout, but somewhat longer at the base; Angora like the brush of a fox, but longer in the hair; Russian equally long in the hair, but more full at the end; tail shorter, rather blunt, like a tassel.	
Size, Shape, and Condition	10

Large, small in bone, looking larger than it really is on account of the length of the hair; body long; legs short; tail carried low, not over the back, which is a fault; fur clean and glossy, even, smooth, and flakey, which gives an appearance of quality.	
Colour	15
Ground colour, deep, rich reddish-brown, more rufous on the nose, ears, mane, and inside the legs and belly; tip of nose red, edged with black; blue, bright, deep, rich, even, dark colour; silver, lighter and equally even tint; and so light gray; and white ground, pure white.	
Markings	15
Jet-black lines, not too broad, scarcely so wide as the ground colour seen between, so as to give a light and brilliant effect. When the black lines are broader than the colour space, it is a defect, being then black marked with colour, instead of colour marked with black. The lines must be clear, sharp, and well-defined, in every way distinct, having no mixture of the ground colour. Head, legs, and tail regularly marked, the latter with rings, the lines on the throat and chest being in no way blurred or broken, but clear, graceful, and continuous; lips, cushions of feet, the backs of the hind-legs and the ear-points black.	
Total	100

In chocolate, mahogany, red, or yellow long-haired tabbies, the markings and colours to be the same as in the short-haired cats; but in points to count the same as the last in all qualities.

Spotted tabbies to count the same in all points, the only difference being that instead of stripes, the cats are marked with clear, well-defined spots.

All fancy colours to be shown in the "any other variety of

colour" class, and judged according to quality of coat, beauty, and rarity of colouring or marking. The small, thin, broken-banded tabby should go in this class, as also those with thin, light, wavy lines.

All foreign, wild, or other cats of peculiar form to go into the class for "any other variety or species."

"Sylvia."

DISEASES OF CATS

Cats, like many other animals, both wild and domestic, are subject to diseases, several being fatal, others yielding to known curatives; many are of a very exhaustive character, some are epidemic, others are undoubtedly contagious—the two worst of these are what is known as the distemper and the mange. Through the kindness of friends I am enabled to give recipes for medicines considered as useful, or, at any rate, tending to abate the severity of the attack in the one, and utterly eradicate the other. Care should always be taken on the first symptoms of illness to remove the animal at once from contact with others. My kind friend, Dr. George Fleming, C.B., principal veterinary surgeon of the army, has courteously sent me a copy of a remedy for cat distemper from his very excellent work, "Animal Plagues: their History, Nature, and Prevention," which I give in full.

CATARRHAL FEVERS.

"Cats are, like some other of the domesticated animals, liable to be attacked by two kinds of Catarrhal Fever, one of which is undoubtedly very infectious—like distemper in dogs—and the other may be looked upon as the result of a simple cold, and therefore not transmissible. The first is, of course, the most severe and fatal, and often prevails most extensively, affecting cats generally over wide areas, sometimes entire continents being invaded by it. From A.D. 1414 up to 1832 no fewer than nineteen widespread outbreaks of this kind have been recorded. The most notable of these was in 1796, when the cats in England and Holland were generally attacked by the disease, and in the following year when it had spread over Europe and extended to America; in 1803, it again appeared in this country and over a large part of the European continent.

"The symptoms are intense fever, prostration, vomiting, diarrhœa, sneezing, cough, and profuse discharge from the nose and eyes. Sometimes the parotid glands are swollen, as in human mumps. Dr. Darwin, of Derby, uncle to Charles Darwin, thought it was a kind of mumps, and therefore designated it *Parotitis felina*.

"The treatment consists in careful nursing and cleanliness, keeping the animal moderately warm and comfortable. The disease rapidly produces intense debility, and therefore the strength should be maintained from the very commencement by frequent small doses of strong beef-tea, into which one grain of quinine has been introduced twice a day, a small quantity of port wine (from half to one teaspoonful) according to the size of the cat, and the state of debility. If there is no diarrhœa, but constipation, a small dose of castor oil or syrup of buckthorn should be given. Solid food should not be allowed until convalescence has set in. Isolation, with regard to other cats, and disinfection, should be attended to.

"Simple Catarrh demands similar treatment. Warmth, cleanliness, broth, and beef-tea, are the chief items of treatment, with a dose of castor oil if constipation is present. If the discharge obstructs the nostrils it should be removed with a sponge, and these and the eyes may be bathed with a weak lotion of vinegar and water."

"As regards inoculation for distemper," Dr. Fleming says, "it has been tried, but the remedy is often worse than the disease, at least as bad as the natural disease. *Vaccination* has also been tried, but it is *valueless*. Probably inoculation with cultivated or modified virus would be found a good and safe preventative."

I was anxious to know about this, as inoculation used to be the practice with packs of hounds.

It will be observed that Dr. Fleming treats the distemper as a kind of influenza, and considers one of the most important things is to keep up the strength of the suffering animal. Other members of the R.C.V.S., whom I have consulted, have all given the same kind of advice, not only prescribing for the sick animal wine, but brandy, as a last resource, to arouse sinking vitality. Mr. George Cheverton, of High Street, Tunbridge Wells, who is very successful with animals and their diseases, thinks it best to treat them homœopathically. The following is what he prescribes as efficacious for some of the most dire complaints with which cats are apt to be afflicted.

WORMS.

For a full-grown cat give 3 grains of santonine every night for a week or 10 days; it might be administered in milk, or given in a small piece of beef or meat of any kind. After the course give an aperient powder.

MANGE.

The best possible remedies for this disease are arsenicum, 2× trituration, and sulphur, 2× trituration, given on alternate days, as much as will lie on a threepenny piece, night and morning, administered as above.

A most useful lotion is acid sulphurous, 1 oz. to 5 oz. of water, adding about a teaspoonful of glycerine, and sponging the affected parts twice or thrice daily.

COLDS.

The symptoms are twofold, usually there is constant sneezing and discharge from the nose. Aconite, 1× tincture, 1 drop given every 3 hours in alternation with arsenicum, 3× trituration, will speedily remove the disease. Should there be stuffing of the nose, and difficult breathing, give mercurius biniod., 3× trituration, a dose every 3 or 4 hours.

COUGHS.

The short, hard, dry cough will always give way to treatment with belladonna, 3× trituration, 3 grains every 3 or 4 hours.

For the difficult breathing, with rattling in the chest and bronchial tubes, with distressing cough, antimonium tartaric., 2×, grains iij every 2, 3 or 4 hours, according to the severity of the symptoms.

DISTEMPER.

Early symptoms should be noted and receive prompt attention; this will often cut short the duration of the malady. The first indications usually are a disinclination to rest in the usual place, seeking a dark corner beneath a sofa, etc. The eyes flow freely, the nose after becoming hard and dry becomes stopped with fluid, the tongue parched, and total aversion to food follows. The breathing becomes short and laboured, the discharges are offensive, and the animal creeps away into some quiet corner to die—if before this its life has not been mercifully ended.

On discovery of *first* symptoms, give 2 drops aconite and arsenicum in alternation every 3 hours. When the nose becomes dry, and the eye restless and glaring, give belladonna.

CANKER OF EAR.

When internal, drop into the affected ear, night and morning, 3 or 5 drops of the following mixture:

Tincture of Hydrastis Canadensis 2 drachms.
Carbolic Acid (pure) ½ "
Glycerine, to make up to 2 oz.

If external, paint with the mixture the affected parts.

APERIENT.

Get a chemist to rub down a medium-size croton bean with about 40 grains of sugar of milk, and divide into four powders. One of these powders given in milk usually suffices. Large cats often require two powders. The dose might be repeated if necessary.

Dose, when drops are ordered, 2 drops.
" " trituration is ordered, 2 to 3 grains.

REMEDIES AND STRENGTHENING MEDICINES.

Aconite, 1× tincture.
Arsenicum, 2× trituration.
Antimonium tartaricum, 2× trituration.
Belladonna, 3× trituration.
Mercurius biniodatus, 3× trituration.
Hydrastis canadensis, [Greek: phi] tincture.
Sulphur, 2× trituration.
Santonine.

Mr. Frank Upjohn, of Castelnau, Barnes, has also kindly forwarded me his treatment of some few of the cat ailments. Mindful of the old proverb that "In a multitude of counsellors there is wisdom," I place all before my friends, and those of the cat, that they may select which remedy they deem best:

DISTEMPER.

Take yellow basilicon, 1 oz.; flowers of sulphur, ½ oz.; oil of juniper, 3 drachms. Mix for ointment. Then give sulphide of mercury, 3 grains, two or three times on alternate nights.

PURGATIVE.

Nothing like castor oil for purgation; half the quantity of syrup of buckthorn, if necessary, may be added.

WORMS.

Two or three grains of santonine in a teaspoonful of castor oil, for two or three days.

CATARRH.

Cold in the eyes and sneezing may be relieved by sweet spirits of nitre, 1 drachm; minocrerus spirit, 3 drachms; antimony wine, 1 drachm; water to 1½ oz. Mix. Give 1 teaspoonful every two or three hours.

FLEAS, AND IRRITATION OF SKIN.

Two drachms pure carbolic acid to 6 oz. of water well mixed for a lotion, and apply night and morning.

EYE OINTMENT.

Red oxide of mercury, 12 grains; spermaceti ointment, 1 oz. Mix.

The above prescription was given to me many years ago by the late Dr. Walsh (Stonehenge), and I have found it of great service, both for my own eyes, also those of animals and birds. Wash the eyes carefully with warm water, dry off with a soft silk handkerchief, and apply a little of the ointment. Dr. Walsh informed me that he deemed it excellent for canker in the ear, but of that I have had no experience.

FOR MANGE.

In the early stages of mange, flowers of sulphur mixed in vaseline, and rubbed in the coat of the cat, is efficacious, giving sulphur in the milk, the water, and on the food of the patient; also give vegetable diet.

Another remedy: give a teaspoonful of castor oil; next day give raw meat, dusted over with flowers of sulphur. Also give sulphur in milk. If there are any sore places, bathe with lotion made from camphorated oil in which some sulphur is mixed. Oil, 2 oz.; camphor, ¼ oz.; sulphur, a teaspoonful.

As a rule, when the animal is of value, either intrinsically or as a pet, the best plan is to consult a practitioner, well versed in the veterinary science and art, especially when the cat appears to suffer from some obscure disease, many of which it is very difficult to detect, unless by the trained and practised eye. Of all the ailments, both of dogs and cats, distemper is the worst to combat, and is so virulent and contagious that I have thought it well to offer remedies that are at least worthy of a trial, though when the complaint has firm hold, and the attack very severe, the case is generally almost hopeless, especially with high-bred animals.

POISON.

It is not generally known that the much-admired laburnum contains a strong poison, and is therefore an exceedingly dangerous plant. All its parts—blossoms, leaves, seeds, even the bark and the roots—are charged with a poison named *cytisin*, which was discovered by Husemann and Marms in 1864.

A small dose of juice infused under the skin is quite sufficient to kill a cat or a dog. Children have died from eating the seeds, of which ten or twelve were sufficient to cause death. The worst of it is that there is *no remedy*, no antidote against this poison. How many cases have happened before the danger was discovered is of course only a matter of conjecture, as few would suspect the cause to come from the lovely plant that so delights the eye.

It has, however, long been known to gamekeepers and others, and used by them to destroy "vermin." When quite a boy I remember an old uncle of mine telling me to beware of it even in gathering the blossom.

THE WILD CAT OF BRITAIN

The wild cat is said to be now extinct in England, and only found in some of the northern parts of Scotland, or the rocky parts of the mountains of the south, where I am informed it may yet occasionally be seen. The drawing I give above was made from one sent to the first Crystal Palace Cat Show in 1871, by the Duke of Sutherland, from Sutherlandshire. It was caught in a trap by the fore-leg, which was much injured, but not so as to prevent its moving with great alacrity, even with agility, endeavouring frequently to use the claws of both fore-feet with a desperate determination and amazing vigour. It was a very powerful animal, possessing great strength, taking size into consideration, and of extraordinary fierceness.

Mr. Wilson, the manager of the show, though an excellent naturalist, tried to get it out of the thick-barred, heavy-made travelling box in which it arrived, into one of the ordinary wire show-cages, thinking it would appear to better advantage; but in this endeavour he was unsuccessful, the animal resisting all attempts to expel it from the one into the other, making such frantic and determined opposition that the idea was abandoned. This was most fortunate, for the wire cages then in use were afterwards found unequal to confining even the ordinary domestic cat, which, in more than one instance, forced the bars apart sufficiently to allow of escape. As it was, the wild cat maintained its position, sullenly retiring to one corner of the box, where it scowled, growled, and fought in a most fearful and courageous manner during the time of its exhibition, never once relaxing its savage watchfulness or attempts to injure even those who fed it. I never saw anything more unremittingly ferocious, nor apparently more untamable.

It was a grand animal, however, and most interesting to the naturalist, being, even then, scarcely ever seen; if so, only in districts far away and remote from the dwellings of civilisation. Yet I believe I saw one among the rocks of Bodsbeck, in Dumfriesshire, many years ago, though of this I am not certain, as it was too far away for accurate observation before it turned and stood at bay, and on my advancing it disappeared. The animal shown at the Crystal Palace was very much lighter in colour, and with less markings than those in the British Museum, the tail shorter, and the dark rings fewer, the lines on the body not much deeper in tint than the ground colour, excepting on the forehead and the inside of the fore-legs, which were darker, rather a light red round the mouth, and almost white on the chest—which appears to be usual with the wild cat; the eyes were yellow-tinted green, the tips of the ears, the lips, cushions of the feet, and a portion of the back part of the hind-legs, black; the markings were, in short, irregular thin lines, and in no way resembled those of the ordinary black-marked domestic tabby cat, possessing little elegance of line—in character it was bolder, having a rugged sturdiness, being stronger and broader built, the fore-arms thick, massive, and endowed with great power, with long, curved claws, the feet were stout, sinewy, and strong; altogether it was a very peculiar, interesting, and extraordinary animal. What became of it I never learned.

In 1871 and 1872, a wild cat was exhibited at the Crystal Palace Cat Show, by the Earl of Hopetoun, aged three years, also some hybrid kittens, the father of which was a long-haired cat, the mother a sandy, by a wild cat out of a long-haired tabby, which proves, if proof were wanting, that such hybrids breed freely either with hybrids, the domestic, or the wild cat.

Mr. Frank Buckland also exhibited a hybrid between the wild and tame cat.

The Zoological Society, a pair of wild cats which did not appear to be British.

In 1873, Mr. A. H. Senger sent a fine specimen of hybrid,

between the domestic cat and Scotch wild cat.

An early description of the wild cat in England is to be found in an old book on Natural History, and copied into a work on "Menageries," "Bartholomœus de Proprietatibus Rerum," which was translated into English by Thomas Berthlet, and printed by Wynkyn de Worde as early as 1498. There is a very interesting description of the cat, which gives nearly all the properties of the wild animal in an odd and very amusing way. It states: "He is most like to the leopard, and hath a great mouthe, and saw teeth and sharp, and long tongue, and pliant, thin, and subtle; and lappeth therewith when he drinketh, as other beasts do, that have the nether lip shorter than the over; for, by cause of unevenness of lips, such beasts suck not in drinking, but lap and lick, as Aristotle saith and Plinius also. And he is a full lecherous beast in youth, swift, pliant, and merry, and leapeth, and riseth on all things that is tofore him; and is led by a straw, and playeth therewith, and is a right heavy beast in age, and full sleepy, and lieth slyly in wait for mice; and is ware where they bene more by smell than by sight, and hunteth and riseth on them in privy places; and when he taketh a mouse, he playeth therewith, and eateth him after the play; and is a cruel beast when he is wild, and dwelleth in woods, and hunteth there small wild beasts as conies and hares."

The next appears in John Bossewell's "Workes of Armorie," folio, A.D. 1597:

"This beaste is called a Musion, for that he is enimie to Myse and Rattes. He is slye and wittie, and seeth so sharpely that he overcommeth darknes of the nighte by the shyninge lyghte of his eyne. In shape of body he is like unto a Leoparde, and hathe a great mouth. He dothe delight that he enioyeth his libertye; and in his youthe he is swifte, plyante, and merye. He maketh a rufull noyse and a gastefull when he profereth to fighte with an other. He is a cruell beaste when he is wilde, and falleth on his owne feete from most high places: and vneth is hurt therewith.

"When he hath a fayre skinne, he is, as it were, prowde thereof, and then he goeth faste aboute to be seene...."

Those who have seen the wild cat of Britain, especially in confinement, will doubtless be ready to endorse this description as being "true to the life," even to the "rufull noyse," or his industry in the way of fighting. Yet even this old chronicler mentions the fact of his being "wilde," clearly indicating a similar animal in a state of domestication. Later on we find Maister Salmon giving an account of the cat in his strangely-curious book, "Salmon's Compleat English Physician; or, the Druggist's Shop Opened," A.D. 1693, in which he relates that marvellous properties exist in the brain, bones, etc., of the cat, giving recipes mostly cruel and incredible. He describes "Catus the Cat" in such terms as these:

"*The Cat of Mountain*, all which are of one nature, and agree much in one shape, save as to their magnitude, the *wild Cat* being larger than the *Tame* and the *Cat of Mountain* much larger than the *wild Cat*. It has a broad Face, almost like a Lyon, short Ears, large Whiskers, shining Eyes, short, smooth Hair, long Tail, rough Tongue, and armed on its Feet, with Claws, being a crafty, subtle, watchful Creature, very loving and familiar with Man-kind, the mortal enemy to the Rat, Mouse, and all sorts of Birds, which it seizes on as its prey. As to its Eyes, Authors say that they shine in the Night, and see better at the full, and more dimly at the change of the moon; as also that the Cat doth vary his Eyes with the Sun, the Apple of its Eye being long at Sun rise, round towards Noon, and not to be seen at all at night, but the whole Eye shining in the night. These appearances of the Cats' Eyes I am sure are true, but whether they answer to the times of the day, I never observed." "Its flesh is not usually eaten, yet in some countries it is accounted an excellent dish."

Mr. Blaine, in his excellent and useful work, the "Encyclopædia of Rural Sports"—a book no sportsman should be without—thus discusses the origin of the domestic cat compared with the British wild cat:

"We have yet, however, to satisfy ourselves with regard to the origin of the true wild cat (*Felis catus*, Linn.), which, following the analogies of the *Felinæ* generally, are almost exclusively native to countries warmer than our own. It is true that occasionally varieties of the *Felinæ* do breed in our caravans and menageries, where artificial warmth is kept up to represent something like a tropical temperature; but the circumstance is too rare to ground any opinion on of their ever having been indigenous here—at least, since our part of the globe has cooled down to its present temperature. It is, therefore, more than probable that both the wild and the tame cat have been derived from some other extra-European source or sources. We say source or sources, for such admission begets another difficulty not easily got over, which is this, that if both of these grimalkins own one common root, in which variety was it that the very marked differences between them have taken place? Most sportsmen, we believe, suspect that they own one common origin, and some naturalists also do the same, contending that the differences observable between them are attributable solely to the long-continued action of external agencies, which had modified the various organs to meet the varied necessities of the animals. The wild cat, according to this theory, having to contend with powerful enemies, expanded in general dimensions; its limbs, particularly, became massive; and its long and strong claws, with the powerful muscular mechanism which operated on them, fitted it for a life of predacity. Thus its increased size enabled it to stand some time before any other dogs than high-bred foxhounds, and even before them also, in any place but the direct open ground. There exist, however, in direct contradiction to this opinion, certain specialities proper to the wild, and certain other to the domestic cat, besides the simple expansion of bulk, which sufficiently disprove their identity. It will be seen that a remarkable difference exists between the tails of the two animals; that of the domestic being, as is well known, long, and tapering elegantly to a point, whereas that of the wild cat is seen to be broad, and to terminate abruptly in a blunt or rounded extremity. Linnæus and Buffon having both of them confounded these two species into one, have contributed much to propagate this error, which affords us another opportunity of adding to the many we have taken of remarking on the vast importance of comparative anatomy, which enables us to draw just distinctions between animals that might otherwise erroneously be adjudged to be dependent on external agencies, etc. Nor need we rest here, for what doubt can be entertained on the subject when we point at the remarkable difference between the intestines of the two? *Those of the domestic are nine times the length of its body*, whereas, in the *wild cat*, they are little more than *three times as long as the body*."

The food of the wild cat is said to consist of animals, and in the opinion of some, fish should be added. Why not also birds' eggs? Cats are particularly fond of the latter. In the event of their finding and destroying a nest, they invariably eat the eggs, and generally the shells.

Much has been written as to the aptitude of the domestic cat at catching fish. If this be so, are fish necessarily a part of the food of the native wild cat? Numerous instances are adduced of our "household cat" plunging into water in pursuit of and capture of fish. Although I have spent much time in watching cats that were roaming beside streams and about ponds, there has never been even an attempt at "fishing." Frogs they will take and kill, often greedily devouring the small ones. Yet doubtless they will hunt, catch, and eat fish, for the fact has become proverbial.

A writer in "Menageries" states: "There is no doubt that wild cats will seize on fish, and the passionate longing of the domestic cat after this food is an evidence of the natural desire. We have seen a cat overcome her natural reluctance to wet her feet, and take an eel out of a pail of water." Dr. Darwin alludes to this propensity: "Mr. Leonard, a very intelligent friend of mine, saw a cat catch a trout by darting on it in deep, clear water, at the Mill, Wexford, near Lichfield. The cat belonged to Mr. Stanley, who had often seen it catch fish."

Wild cat, British Museum.

Cases have also been known of cats catching fish in shallow water, springing on them from the banks of streams and ponds; but I take this as not *the habit* of the domestic cat, though it is not unusual.

Gray, in a poem, tells of a cat's death through drowning, while attempting to take gold-fish from a vase filled with water.

Of Dr. Samuel Johnson it is related, that his cat having fallen sick and refused all food, he became aware that cats are fond of fish. With this knowledge before him he went to the fishmonger's and bought an oyster for the sick creature, wrapped it in paper and brought the appetising morsel home. The cat relished the dainty food, and the Doctor was seen going on the same kindly errand every day until his suffering feline friend was restored to health.

Still this is no proof that the *wild* cat, in a pure state of nature, feeds on fish. Again, it is nothing unusual for domestic cats to catch and eat cockroaches, crickets, cockchafers, also large and small moths, but not so all. In domesticity some are almost omnivorous. But is the wild cat? Taking its anatomical structure into consideration, there is doubtless a wide distinction, both as regards food and habit.

In Daniel's "Rural Sports," A.D. 1813, the wild cat is stated to be "now scarce in England, inhabiting the mountainous and woody parts. Mr. Pennant describes it as *four* times the size of the house cat, but the head larger, that it multiplies as fast, and may be called the British *tiger*, being the fiercest and most destructive beast we have. When only wounded with shot they will attack the person who injured them, and often have strength enough to be no despicable enemy."

Through the kind courtesy of that painstaking, excellent, observant, and eminent naturalist, Mr. J. E. Harting, I am enabled to reprint a portion of his lecture on the origin of the domestic cat, and which afterwards appeared in *The Field*. Although many of the statements are known to naturalists, still I prefer giving them in the order in which they are so skilfully arranged, presenting, as they do, a very garland of facts connected with the British wild cat (*Felis catus*) up to the present, and which I deem valuable from many points of view, but the more particularly as a record of an animal once abundant in England, where it has now apparently almost, if not quite, ceased to exist.

"In England in former days, the wild cat was included amongst the beasts of chase, and is often mentioned in royal grants giving liberty to inclose forest land and licence to hunt there (extracts from several such grants will be found in the *Zoologist* for 1878, p. 251, and 1880, p. 251). Nor was it for diversion alone that the wild cat was hunted. Its fur was much used as trimming for dresses, and in this way was worn even by nuns at one time. Thus, in Archbishop Corboyle's 'Canons,' anno 1127, it is ordained 'that no abbess or nun use more costly apparel than such as is made of lambs' or *cats'* skins,' and as no other part of the animal but the skin was of any use here, it grew into a proverb that 'You can have nothing of a cat but her skin.'

"The wild cat is believed to be now extinct, not only in England and Wales, but in a great part of the south of Scotland. About five years ago a Scottish naturalist resident in Stirlingshire (Mr. J. A. Harvie Brown) took a great deal of trouble, by means of printed circulars addressed to the principal landowners throughout Scotland and the Isles, to ascertain the existing haunts of the wild cat in that part of the United Kingdom. The result of his inquiries, embodying some very interesting information, was published in the *Zoologist* for January, 1881. The replies which he received indicated pretty clearly, although perhaps unexpectedly, that there are now no wild cats in Scotland south of a line drawn from Oban on the west coast up the Brander Pass to Dalmally, and thence following the borders of Perthshire to the junction of the three counties of Perth, Forfar and Aberdeen, northward to Tomintoul, and so to the city of Inverness. We are assured that it is only to the northward and westward of this line that the animal still keeps a footing in suitable localities, finding its principal shelter in the great deer forests. Thus we see that the wild cat is being gradually driven northward before advancing civilisation and the increased supervision of moors and forests. Just as the reindeer in the twelfth century was driven northward from England and found its last home in Caithness, and as the wolf followed it a few centuries later, so we may expect one day that the wild cat will come to be numbered amongst the 'extinct British animals.'

"A recent writer in the new edition of the 'Encyclopædia Britannica' (art. *Cat*) expresses the opinion that the wild cat still exists in Wales and in the north of England, but gives no proof of its recent occurrence there. From time to time we see reports in the newspapers to the effect that a wild cat has been shot or trapped in some out-of-the-way part of the country; but it usually turns out to be a large example of the domestic cat, coloured like the wild form. It is remarkable that when cats in England are allowed to return to a feral state, their offspring, in the course of generations, show a tendency to revert to the wild type of the country; partly, no doubt, in consequence of former interbreeding with the wild species when the latter was common throughout all the wooded portions of the country, and partly because the light-coloured varieties of escaped cats, being more readily seen and destroyed, are gradually eliminated, while the darker wild type is perpetuated. The great increase in size observable in the offspring of escaped domestic cats is no doubt due to continuous living on freshly-killed, warm-blooded animals, and to the greater use of the muscles which their new mode of life requires. In this way I think we may account for the size and appearance of the so-called 'wild cats' which are from time to time reported south of the Tweed.

"Perhaps the last genuine wild cat seen in England was the one shot by Lord Ravensworth at Eslington, Northumberland, in 1853;[A] although so recently as March, 1883, a cat was shot in Bullington Wood, Lincolnshire, which in point of size, colour, and markings was said to be quite indistinguishable from the wild *Felis catus*. Bullington Wood is one of an almost continuous chain of great woodlands, extending from Mid-Lincolnshire to near Peterborough. Much of the district has never been preserved for game, and keepers are few and far between; hence the wild animals have enjoyed an almost complete immunity from persecution. Cats are known to have bred in these woods in a wild state for generations, and there is no improbability that the cat in question may have descended directly from the old British wild cat. Under all the circumstances, however, it seems more likely to be a case of reversion under favourable conditions from the domestic to the wild type.

"In Ireland, strange to say, notwithstanding reports to the contrary, all endeavours to find a genuine wild cat have failed, the so-called 'wild cat' of the natives proving to be the 'marten cat,' a very different animal.

"We thus come back to the question with which we started, namely, the question of origin of the domestic cat; and the conclusion, I think, at which we must arrive is, that although *Felis catus* has contributed to the formation of the existing race of domestic cats, it is not the sole ancestor. Several wild species of Egyptian and Indian origin having been ages ago reclaimed, the interbreeding of their offspring and crossing with other wild species in the countries to which they have been at various times exported, has resulted in the gradual production of the many varieties, so different in shape and colour, with which we are now familiar."

Before quitting the subject, I would point to the fact that when the domestic cat takes to the woods and becomes wild, it becomes much larger, stronger, and changes in colour; and there can be little doubt that during the centuries of the existence of the cat in England there must have been numberless crosses and intercrosses, both with regard to the *males* of the domestic cat as with wild *females*, and *vice versâ*; yet the curious fact remains that the wild cat still retains its peculiar colouring and form, as is shown by the skins preserved in the British Museum and elsewhere.

Mr. Darwin, in his "Voyage of the Beagle," 1845 (p. 120), in his notes of the first colonists of La Plata, A.D. 1535, says, among other animals that he saw was "the common cat altered into a *large* and *fierce* animal, inhabiting the rocky hills," etc.

Another point on which I wish to give my impressions is the act of the cat in what is termed "sharpening its claws." Mr. Darwin notes certain trees where the jaguars "*sharpen their claws*," and mentions the scars were of different ages; he also thought they did this "*to tear off the horny points*." This, I believe, is the received opinion among naturalists; but I differ *entirely* from this view of the practice. It is a fact, however, and worthy of notice, that all cats do so, even the domestic cat. I had *one* of the legs of a kitchen table entirely torn to pieces by my cats; and after much observation I came to the conclusion that it has nothing whatever to do with *sharpening* the claws, but is done to stretch the muscles and tendons of the feet so that they work readily and strongly, as the retraction of the claws for lengthened periods must tend to contract the tendons used for the purpose of extending or retracting; therefore the cats fix the points of their claws in something soft, and bear downwards with the whole weight of the body, simply to stretch and, by use, to strengthen the ligatures that pull the claws forward. It is also to be noted that even the domestic cat goes to one particular place or tree to insert the claws and drag forward the muscles—perhaps even in the leather of an arm-chair, a costly practice. Why one object is always selected is that they may not betray their presence by numerous marks in the neighbourhood, if wild, to other animals or their enemies. I have mentioned this to my brother, John Jenner Weir, F.L.S., and he concurs with me throughout.

I find in Strutt's "Sports and Pastimes" that of the names applied to companies of animals in the Middle Ages, several are still in use, though many have become obsolete; and also a few of the beasts have ceased to exist in a wild state. Some were very curious, such as a *skulk* of foxes, a *cete* of badgers, a *huske* or *down* of hares, a *nest* of rabbits, and a *clowder of cats*, and a *kindle of young cats*. Now cats are said to *kitten*, and rabbits *kindle*.

The following shows the value of the cat nearly a thousand years ago; it is to be found in Bewick's "Quadrupeds": "In the time of Hoel the Good, King of Wales, who died in the year 948, laws were made as well to preserve as to fix the different prices of animals; among which the cat is included, as being at that period of great importance, on account of its scarcity and utility.

"The price of a kitten, before it could see, was fixed at one penny; till proof could be given of its having caught a mouse, twopence; after which it was rated at fourpence, which was a great sum in those days, when the value of specie was extremely high. It was likewise required that it should be perfect in its sense of hearing and seeing, should be a good mouser, have its claws whole, and, if a female, be a careful nurse. If it failed in any of these good qualities, the seller was to forfeit to the buyer a third part of its value. If any one should steal or kill a cat that guarded the Prince's granary, he was either to forfeit a milch ewe, her fleece and lamb, or as much wheat as when poured on the cat suspended by its feet (its head touching the floor), would form a heap high enough to cover the tip of the former." Bewick remarks: "Hence we may conclude that cats were not originally natives of these islands, and from the great care taken to improve the breed of this prolific creature, we may suppose were but little known at that period."

I scarcely think this the right conclusion, the English wild cat being anatomically different. In Hone's popular works it is stated that "Cats are supposed to have been brought into England from the island of Cyprus by some foreign merchants, who came hither for tin." Mr. Hone further says: "Wild cats were kept by our ancient kings for hunting. The officers who had charge of these cats seem to have had appointments of equal consequence with the masters of the king's hounds; they were called *Catatores*."

Beaumont and Fletcher in *The Scornful Lady* allude to the hunting of cats in the line,

> "Bring out the *cat-hounds*,
> I'll make you take a tree."

But although large and ferocious, the wild cat was not considered a match for some of the lesser animals, for in Salmon's "English Physician," 1693, we read that "The weasel is an enemy to ravens, crows, and *cats*, and although cats may sometimes set upon them, yet they can scarcely overcome them."

Nevertheless, we find in Daniel's "Rural Sports," 1813, that "*Wild cats* formerly were an object of *sport* to huntsmen. Thus, Gerard Camvile, 6 John, had special licence to hunt the hare, fox, and wild cat, throughout all the King's *forests*; and 23 Henry III., Earl Warren, by giving Simon de Pierpont a *goshawk*, obtained leave to hunt the buck, doe, hart, hind, hare, fox, goat, *cat*, or any other wild beast, in certain lands of Simon's. But it was not for diversion alone that this animal was pursued; for the *skin* was much used by the nuns in their habits, as a *fur*."

Still it appears from Mr. Charles Darwin's "Voyage of the Beagle," that tastes vary. "Doctor Shaw was laughed at for stating the flesh of the lion is in great esteem, having no small affinity with veal, both in the colour, taste, and flavour. Such certainly is the case with the puma. The Guachos differ in their opinion whether the jaguar is good eating; but were unanimous in saying the *cat* is *excellent*."

It is also stated that the Chinese fatten and eat cats with considerable relish; but of this I can obtain no reliable information, some of my friends from China not having heard of the custom, if such it is.

Again referring to the skin of the cat, *vide* Strutt: "In the thirty-seventh year of the reign of Edward III., it was decreed, after enumerating the various kinds of cloth that were to be worn by the nobles, knights, dames, and others, that(Article 2) tradesmen, artificers, and men in office, called yeomen, their wives and children, shall wear no kind of furs excepting those of lambs, of rabbits, of *cats*, and of foxes." Further: "No man, unless he be possessed of the yearly value of forty shillings, shall wear any furs but black and white lambs' skins." Lambs' and cats' skins were equivalent in value and order.

In the twenty-second year of this monarch's reign, all the former statutes "against excess in apparel" were repealed.

My old friend Fairholt, in his useful work on costume, says of the Middle Ages: "The peasants wore cat skins, badger skins, etc."

One of the reasons why the skin of cats was used on cloaks and other garments for trimming, being that it showed humility in dress, and not by way of affectation or vanity, but for warmth and comfort, it being of the lowest value of any, with the exception of lambs' skin and badgers'; and adopted by some priests as well as nuns, when wishing to impress others with their deep sense of humility in all things, even to their wearing-apparel. The proof of which Strutt's "Habits of the Anglo-Normans," *circâ* twelfth century, fully illustrates:

"William of Malmesbury, speaking of Wulfstan, Bishop of Worcester, assures us that he avoided all appearance of pride and ostentation in his dress, and though he was very wealthy, he never used any furs finer than lambs' skin for the lining of his garments. Being blamed for such needless humility by Geoffrey, Bishop of Constans, who told him that 'He not only could afford, but even ought to wear those of sables, of beavers, or of foxes,' he replied: 'It may indeed be proper for you politicians, skilful in the affairs of the world, to adorn yourselves in the skins of such cunning animals; but for me, who am a plain man, and not subject to change my opinion, the skins of lambs are quite sufficient.' 'If,' returned his opponent, 'the finer furs are unpleasant, you might at least make use of those of the cat.' 'Believe me,' answered the facetious prelate, 'the lamb of God is much oftener sung in the Church than the cat of God.' This witty retort put Geoffrey to the blush, and threw the whole company into a violent fit of laughter."

Of a very different character was the usage of the cat at clerical festivals. In Mill's "History of the Crusades," one reads with some degree of horror that "In the Middle Ages the cat was a very important personage in religious festivals. At Aix, in Provence, on the festival of the Corpus Christi, the finest he-cat of the country, wrapped like a child in swaddling clothes, was exhibited in a magnificent shrine to public admiration. Every knee was bent, every hand strewed flowers or poured incense; and pussy was treated in all respects as the god of the day. On the festival, however, of St. John (June 24), the poor cat's fate was reversed. A number of cats were put in a wicker basket, and thrown alive into the midst of a large fire, kindled in the public square by the bishop and his clergy. Hymns and anthems were sung, and processions were made by the priests and people in honour of the sacrifice."

While the foregoing was about being printed, Mr. Edward Hamilton, M.D., writing to *The Field*, May 11th, 1889, gives information of a wild cat being shot in Inverness-shire. I therefore insert the paragraph, as every record of so scarce an animal is of importance and value, especially when it is descriptive. He states: "A fine specimen of the wild cat (*Felis sylvestris*) was sent to me on May 3rd, trapped in Inverness-shire on the Ben Nevis range. It was too much decomposed to exhibit. Its dimensions were: from nose to base of tail, 1 foot 11 inches; length of tail, 1 foot; height at shoulder, 1 foot 2 inches; the length of small intestine, 1 foot 8½ inches; and the large intestine, 1 foot 1 inch." It will be seen by these measurements that the animal was not so large as some that have been taken, though excelling in size many of the domestic varieties.

CONCERNING CATS

Cat.—Irish, *Cat*; French, *Chat*; Dutch, *Kat*; Danish, *Kat*; Swedish, *Katt*; German, *Katti* or *Katze*; Latin, *Catus*; Italian, *Gatto*; Portuguese and Spanish, *Gato*; Polish, *Kot*; Russian, *Kots*; Turkish, *Keti*; Welsh, *Cath*; Cornish, *Kath*; Basque, *Catua*; Armenian, *Gaz* or *Katz*. In Armenic, *Kitta*, or *Kaita*, is a male cat.

Abram cat.—This I first thought simply meant a male cat; but I find in Nares, "Abram" is the corruption of "auburn," so, no doubt, a red or sandy tabby cat is intended.

A Wheen cat, a Queen cat (Catus femina).—"Queen" was used by the Saxons to signify the female sex, in that "queen fugol" was used for "hen fowl." Farmers in Kent and Sussex used also to call heifers "little queens."

Carl cat.—A boar or he-cat, from the old Saxon carle or karle, a male, and cat.

Cat.—It was used to denote "Liberty." No animal is more impatient of restriction or confinement, nor yet *seeming* to bear it with more resignation. The Romans made their goddess of Liberty holding a cup in one hand and a broken sceptre in the other, with a cat lying at her feet. Among the goddesses, Diana is said to have assumed the form of a cat. The Egyptians worshiped the cat as an emblem of the moon, not only because it was more active after sunset, but from the dilation and contraction of its orb, symbolical of the waxing and waning of the night goddess. But Bailey, in his dictionary, says cats see best as the sun approaches, and that their eyesight decays as it goes down in the evening. Yet, "on this account," says Mr. Thiselton Dyer, in his "English Folk-lore," "it was so highly esteemed as to receive sacrifices, and even to have stately temples erected to its honour. Whenever a cat died, Brand tells us, all the family shaved their eyebrows; and Diodorus Siculus relates that a Roman happening accidentally to kill a cat, the mob immediately gathered round the house where he was, and neither the entreaties of some principal men by the king, nor the fear of the Romans, with whom the Egyptians were then negotiating a peace, could save the man's life. In so much esteem also was it held, that on the death of its owner the favourite cat, or even kitten, was sacrificed, embalmed, and placed in the same sarcophagus."

Some few years ago, Mr. E. Long, R.A., exhibited at the Royal Academy a very fine picture of Egyptians idol-making, idol worshippers and sellers; the lines from Juvenal being descriptive:

> "All know what monsters Egypt venerates;It worships
> crocodiles, or it adoresThe snake-gorged ibis; and
> sacred apeGraven in gold is seen ...Whole cities
> prayTo *cats* and fishes, or the dog invoke."

Cat.—A metal tripod for holding a plate or Dutch oven before the fire. So called because, in whatever position it is placed, it is supported by the spokes; as it is said a cat will always light on its feet, so the plate-holder will stand firmly in any position. These old brass appliances have now gone out of use and are seldom seen, the new mode of "handing round" not requiring them. Another reason, doubtless, is the lowness of the fire compared with the stove of former years, which was high up in the bygone "parlour grate."

Cat.—A cross old woman was called "a cat"; or to a shrewish, the epithet was applied tauntingly.

> "But will you woo this wild cat?"
> *Taming of the Shrew, Act I., Scene 2.*

Cat.—A ship formed on the Norwegian model, having a narrow stern, projecting quarters, and a deep waist. It is strongly built, from four to six hundred tons' burden, and employed in the coal trade.

Cat.—A strong tackle, or combination of pulleys, to hook and draw in the anchor perpendicularly up to the cat-head of the ship.

Cat.—A small kind of anchor is sometimes called a cat or ketch; by the Dutch, "Kat."

Cat.—"At the edge of the moat, opposite the wooden tower, a strong penthouse, which they called a 'cat,' might be seen stealing towards the curtain, and gradually filling up the moat with facines and rubbish."—Read *Cloister and Hearth*, chap, xliii. (Davis' "Glossary.")

Catacide.—A cat-killer (Bailey, 1726).

Catamount.—Cat of the mountain, the ordinary wild cat, when found on the mountains, among the rocks or woods.

Cat and trap.—A game or play (Ainsworth). This is probably that known as "trap, bat, and ball," as on striking the trap, after the ball is placed on the lever, it is propelled upwards, and then struck by the batsman.

Catapult.—A military engine for battering or attacking purposes. A modern toy, by which much mischief and evil is done by unthinking boys.

Cat-bird.—An American bird, whose cry resembles that of a cat, the *Turdus felivox*.

Cat-block.—A two or threefold block with an iron strap and large hook, used to draw up an anchor to the cat-head.

Cat-call.—"A tin whistle. The ancients divided their dramas into four parts: *pro'tasis* (introduction), *epit'asis* (continuation), *catas'tasis* (climax), and *catas'trophë* (conclusion or *dénouement*). The cat-call is the call for the cat or *catastrophe*."—Brewer's *Dictionary of Phrase and Fable*.

"Sound, sound, ye viols; be the cat-call dumb."

Dunciade, I. 303.

The modern imitation of "cat-calls" is caused by whistling with two fingers in the mouth, and so making an intensely shrill noise, with waulings imitating "catterwaulings." Also a shrill tin whistle, round and flat, set against the teeth.

Cat-eaten Street.—In London; properly "Catte Street" (Stow).

Caterpillar.—"*Catyrpelwyrm* among fruit" is corrupted from old French *Chatte peleuse* (Palsgrave, 1530). "Hairy cat;" the last part of the word was probably assimilated to *piller*, a robber or despoiler (Palmer's *Folk Etymology*).

Caterwauling.—The wrawl of cats in rutting times; any hideous noise. Topsel gives *catwralling*, to "wrall;" "wrawl," to rail or quarrel with a loud voice; hence the Yorkshire expression, "raising a wrow," meaning a row or quarrel. There is also the archaic adjective *wraw* (angry). Caterwaul, therefore, is the wawl or wrawl of cats; the *er* being either a plural, similar to "childer" (children), or a corrupted genitive.—Brewer's *Dictionary of Phrase and Fable.*

"What a caterwawling do you keep here!"
Shakespeare, Twelfth Night, Act II., Scene 3.

"To yawl.—To squall or scream harshly like an enraged cat."
—Holloway (Norfolk).

"Thou must be patient; we came crying hither;
Thou knowest the first time that we smell air,
We *waul* and cry."
King John, Act IV.

Cat-eyed.—Sly, gray eyes, or with large pupils, watchful.

Cat-fall.—A rope used in ships for hoisting the anchor to the cat-head.

Catfish.—A species of the squalus, or shark (*Felis marinus*). The catfish of North America is a species of *cottus*, or bull-head.

Catgut.—A corruption of "gut-cord." The intestines of a sheep, twisted and dried; not that of a cat, as generally supposed. Also, it is stated by some, the finer strings for viols were made from the cat. Mr. Timbs says the original reading in Shakespeare was "*calves'*-gut." "A sort of linen or canvas with wide interstices."—Webster.

Cat-hamed., or *hammed.*—Awkward; sometimes applied to a horse with weak hind-legs, and which drops suddenly behind on its haunches, as a cat is said to do.

Cat-handed.—A Devonshire term for awkward.

Cat-harpings.—"Rope sewing to brace in the shrouds of the lower masts behind their respective yards, to tighten the shrouds and give more room to draw in the yards when the ship is close hauled."—*Marine Dictionary.*

Cat-harping fashion.—Drinking crossways, and not as usual, over the left thumb. Sea term.—Grose.

Cat-head.—"A strong beam, projecting horizontally over the ship's bows, carrying two or three sheaves, above which a rope, called the cat-fall, passes, and communicates with the cat-block."—*Marine Dictionary.*

Cathood.—The time when a kitten is full grown, it is then a cat and has attained maturity, that is, cathood.

Cat-hook.—A strong hook fitted to the cat-block.

Cat-lap.—Weak tea, only fit for the cat to lap, or thin milk and water. In Kent and Sussex it is also often applied to small, *very* small beer; even thin gruel is called "cat-lap." Weak tea is also called "scandal-broth."

Cat-like.—Stealthy, slow, yet appertaining more to appearance.

Catlings.—Down, or moss, growing about walnut-trees, resembling the hair of a cat.

Cat o' Nine Tails.—So called from being nine pieces of cord put together, in each cord nine knots; and this, when used vigorously, makes several long marks not unlike the clawing or scratching of a cat, producing crossing and re-crossing wounds; a fearful and severe punishment, formerly too often exercised for trivial offences.

Cat or *dog wool.*—"Of which cotte or coarse blankets were formerly made" (Bailey). "Cot gase" (refuse wool). "Cat" no doubt was a corruption of "cot."

Cat-pear.—A pear, shaped like a hen's egg, that ripens in October.

Cat pellet.—The pop-gun of boys, one pellet of paper driving out the other. Davis in his "Glossary" thinks it means "tip-cat." Probably it may be the sharpened piece of wood, not the game, that is different altogether, he quotes.

"Who beats the boys from cat pellet, and stool ball."
British Bellman, 1648.

Cat-salt.—A salt obtained from butter.

Cat-salt.—"A sort of salt beautifully granulated, formed out of the bittern or leach brine, used for making hard soap."— *Encyclopædia.*

Cat's-eye.—A precious stone, resembling, when polished, the eye of a cat. It has lately become fashionable.

A large collection of Burmese, Indian, and Japanese curiosities was lately sold by auction. The great attraction of the sale was "The Hindoo Lingam God," consisting of a chrysoberyl *cat's-eye* fixed in a topaz, and mounted in a pyramidal base studded with diamonds and precious stones. This curious relic stood 2¼ inches in height. It was preserved for more than a thousand years in an ancient temple at Delhi, where acts of devotion were paid before it by women anxious to have children. The base is of solid gold, and around it are set nine gems or charms, a diamond, ruby, sapphire, *chrysoberyl cat's-eye*, coral, pearl, hyacinthine garnet, yellow sapphire, and emerald. Round the apex of this gold pyramid is a plinth set with diamonds. On the apex is a topaz 1 10-16ths inch in length, and 9-16ths of an inch in depth, shaped like a horseshoe; in the centre of the horseshoe the *great chrysoberyl cat's-eye* stands upright. This is 15-16ths of an inch in height, and dark brown in colour, and shaped like a pear. An

208

extremely mobile opalescent light crosses the length of the stone in an oblique direction. When Bad Shah Bahadoor Shah, the last King of Delhi, was captured and exiled to the Andaman Isles, his Queen secreted this gem, and it was never seen again until, being distressed during the Mutiny, she sold it to the present owner. The gem was finally knocked down at £2,450 to Mr. S. J. Phillips, jeweller, New Bond Street.

Cat's-foot.—To live under the cat's foot, to be under the dominion of a wife, hen-pecked.

Cat's-foot.—A plant of the genus *Glechoma pes felinus*, ground ivy or gill.

Cat's-head apple.—A large culinary apple, considered by some in form to bear a resemblance to a cat's head. Philips in his poem "Cyder" thus describes it:

> " ...The cat's head's weighty orb,Enormous
> in growth, for various use."

Cat-silver.—An old popular name for mica or talc.

Cat-sleep.—A light doze, a watchful sleep, like that of a hare or of a cat who sits in front of a mouse-hole, a dozy or a sleeping wakefulness.

Cat's-paw.—Any one used by another for getting them out of a difficulty, and for no other reason, is made a cat's-paw of. The simile is from the fable of the monkey using the cat's paw to take his chestnuts out of the fire. A light breeze just ruffling the water in a calm is called a cat's-paw. Also a particular kind of turn in the bight of a rope made to hook tackle on.

Cat's-tail. (Typha latifolia).—A kind of reed which bears a spike like the tail of a cat, which some call reed mace; its long, flat leaves are much used for the bottoms of chairs.

Cats'-tails.—Mares' tails (*equisetum*).

Cat-stane.—"Battle-stone. A monolith in Scotland (sometimes falsely called a Druidical stone). The Norwegian term, banta stein, means the same thing. Celtic—*cath* (battle)."—Brewer's

Dictionary of Phrase and Fable.

Cat-sticks.—Thin legs; compared to the thin sticks with which boys play at cat (Grose).

Catsup or *ketchup.*—A corruption of the Eastern name of "Kitjap." Is then the syllable "cat" a pun on "kit" or "kitten" (a young cat)? Surely not.

Cattaria.—*Nepeta Cattaria. Mentha felina,* the herb cat-mint.

Cattery.—A place where cats are kept, the ordinary name when a person keeps a collection of cats.

Cattish.—Having stealthy ways, slow and cautious in movements, watchful.

Catwater. (Plymouth).—"This is a remarkable instance of mistranslation. The castle at the mouth of the Plym used to be called the Château; but some one, thinking it would be better to Anglicise the French, divided the word into two parts: *chat* (cat), *eau* (water)."—Brewer's *Dictionary of Phrase and Fable.*

Catwhin.—*Rosa spinosissima.* Burnet Rose is the name of the plant.

Cat with two tails.—The earwig. *Northumberland*; Holloway.

Gil cat.—A male cat; some say an old male. Nares says, an expression exactly analogous to "Jack ass;" the one being formerly called "Gil" or "Gilbert," as commonly as the other "Jack." "Tom cat" is now the usual term, and for a similar reason. "Tibert" is said to be the old French for "Gilbert." From "Tibert," "Tib," "Tibby," also was a common name for a cat. Wilkins, in his "Index to Philosophical Language," has "Gil" (male) cat in the same way as a male cat is called a "Tom" cat. In some counties the cock fowl is called a "Tom." It is unknown whence the origin of the latter term.

Grimalkin.—Poetical name for a cat (Bailey). "Mawkin" signifies a hare in Scotland (Grose). In Sussex a hare is often called "puss" or "pussy." "Puss" is also a common name for a cat.

Grinagog, the cat's uncle.—A foolish, grinning fellow. One who grins without reason (Grose). In Norfolk, if one say "she," the reply is, "Who's 'she'? The cat's aunt?"

Hang me in a bottle like a cat.—"Benedict. If I do, hang me in a bottle like a cat, and shoot at me, and he that hits me, let him be clapt on the shoulder and called Adam" (meaning Adam Bell, the famous archer).—*Much Ado About Nothing*, Act I.

A note in the "Percy Reliques," vol. i., 1812, states: "Bottles were formerly of leather, though perhaps a wooden bottle might be here meant. It is still a diversion in Scotland (1812) to hang up a cat in a small cask or firkin, half filled with soot, and then a parcel of clowns on horseback try to beat out the ends of it, in order to show their dexterity in escaping before the contents fall on them."

From "Demandes Joyeuses" (amusing questions), 1511:

"*Q.* What is that that never was and never will be?
"*A.* A mouse nest in a cat's ear.
"*Q.* Why does a cat cross the road?
"*A.* Because it wants to get to the other side."

Mrs. Evans.—"A local name for a she-cat, owing, it is said, to a witch of the name of Evans, who assumed the appearance of a cat."—Grose.

Nine lives like a cat.—"Cats, from their great suppleness and aptitude to fall on their feet, are commonly said to have nine lives; hence Ben Jonson, in 'Every Man in His Humour,' says: "Tis a pity you had not ten lives—a cat's and your own.'"—Thiselton Dyer's *English Folk-lore.*

"Tyb. What wouldst thou have with me? Mer. Good
king of cats, nothing but one of your nine lives."
Romeo and Juliet, III. I.

Middleton says in "Blurt Master Constable," 1602:

"They have nine lives apiece, like a woman."

Pussy cats.—Male blossom of the willow.

Salt-cat, or *salt-cate.*—A mixture of salt, gravel, clay, old mortar, cumin seed, ginger, and other ingredients, in a pan, which is placed in pigeon lofts.

Sick as a Cat.—Cats are subject to sickness or vomiting for the purpose of throwing up indigestible matter, such as the fur of mice, feathers of birds, which would otherwise collect and form balls internally. For this reason they eat grass, which produces the desired effect; hence arises the phrase "as sick as a cat."

Tabby.—"An old maid; either from Tabitha, a formal antiquated name, or else from a tabby cat; old maids, by the rude, weak-minded, and vulgar, being often compared to cats. 'To drive tab,' to go out on a party of pleasure with wife and family."—Grose's *Glossary.*

> "The neighbour's old cat often
>   Came to pay us a visit
> We made her a bow and courtesy,
>   Each with a compliment in it.
> After her health we asked,
>   Our care and regard to evince;
> (We have made the very same speeches
>   To many an old cat since)."

Mrs. B. Browning
(translation of "Heine").

Tip-cat.—A pleasant game for those engaged in it; not so, too often, for others, medical reports of late tending to show that many cases of the loss of sight have occurred.

To turn Cat in Pan.—This phrase has been a source of much contention, and many different derivations have been given; but all tend to show that it means a complete *turn over*, that is, to quit one side and go to the other, to turn traitor, to turncoat. "To turn cat in pan: *Prævaricor*" (Ainsworth). Bacon, in his Essays "On Cunning," p. 81, says: "There is a cunning which

212

we in England call 'the turning of the cat in the pan,' which is when that a man says to another, 'he lays it as if another had said it to him.'" This is somewhat obscure in definition. Toone says: "The proverbial expression, 'to turn a cat in a pan,' denotes a sudden change in one's party, or politics, or religion, for the sake of being in the ascendant, as a cat always comes down on its legs, however thrown." The Vicar of Bray is quoted as simply a "turncoat," but this does *not* affect the argument. I quite think, and in this others agree with me, that it has nothing to do with the *cat*, but was originally cate. In olden times, and until lately, it was the custom *to toss* pancakes (to turn them over). It was no easy matter; frequently the *cake* or *cate* went in the fire or lodged in the chimney. To turn the cat or cate in the pan was to toss and *turn it completely over*, that is, from one side to the other. The meaning given to the phrase *helps to prove* this view. I merely introduce this because so many have asked for an explanation as regards "the *cat* in pan." I consider the "far-fetched" origins of the term are complete errors. It was a custom to toss pancakes on Shrove Tuesday, and it required great skill to do it well, cleanly, and completely. Some cooks were noted for it, and thought clever if it was done without injury to themselves or clothes.

It appears from "The Westmoreland Dialect," by A. Walker (1790), that cock-fighting and "casting" of pancakes were then common in that county, thus: "Whaar ther wor tae be cock-feightin', for it war pankeak Tuesday," and "we met sum lads an' lasses gangin' to kest (cast) their pankeaks."

To whip the cat.—"To practise the most pinching parsimony, grudging even the scraps and orts, or remnants of food given to the cat."—Holloway (*Norfolk*).

A phrase applied to the village tailor going round from house to house for work.

"To be drunk."

—*Heywood's Philoconothista, 1635, p. 60.*

An itinerant parson is said to "whip the cat."

"A trick practised on ignorant country fellows, vain of their strength, by laying a wager with them that they may be pulled through a pond by a cat. The bet being made, a rope is fixed round the waist of the party to be catted, and the end thrown across the pond, to which the cat is also fastened by a pack-thread, and three or four sturdy fellows are appointed to lead and 'whip the cat.' These, on a signal being given, seize the end of the cord, and, pretending to whip the cat, haul the astonished booby through the water."—Grose, 1785.

The following are culled from the well-known and useful book, Jamieson's "Scottish Dictionary":

Cat.—A small bit of rag, rolled up and put between the handle of a pot and the hook which suspends it over the fire, to raise it a little.—*Roxb.*

Cat.—A handful of straw, with or without corn upon it, or of reaped grain, laid on the ground by the reaper without being put into a sheaf (*Roxb., Dumfr.*). Perhaps from the Belg. word *katt-en,* to throw, the handful of corn being cast on the ground; whence *kat,* a small anchor.

Cat.—The name given to a bit of wood, a horn, or anything which is struck in place of a ball in certain games.

To Cat a Chimney.—To enclose a vent by the process called *Cat and Clay (Teviotd.).*

Cat and Clay.—The materials of which a mud wall is constructed in many parts of S. Straw and clay are well wrought together, and being formed into pretty large rolls, are laid between the different wooden posts by means of which the wall is formed, and carefully pressed down so as to incorporate with each other, or with the twigs that are sometimes plaited from one post to another (*S.*).

Cat and Dog.—The name of an ancient sport (*S.*). It seems to be an early form of *Cricket.* (Query, is this the same as Cat and Trap?)

Catband.—1. The name given to the strong hook used on the

inside of a door or gate, which, being fixed to the wall, keeps it shut. 2. A chain drawn across a street for defence in time of war. Germ., *kette*, a chain, and *band*.

Cat-fish, Sea-cat.—The sea-wolf (S.). *Anarhicas lupus* (Linn.) Sw., *haf-cat*—*i.e.* sea-cat.—Sibbald.

Cat-gut.—Thread fucus, or sea laces. *Fucus filum* (Linn.), *Orkney,* "Neill's Tour."

Cat-Harrow.—"*They draw the Cat-Harrow*"—that is, they thwart one another.—*Loth. Ang.*, Lyndsey.

Cat-heather.—A finer species of heath, low and slender, growing more in separate, upright stalks than the common heath, and flowering only at the top (*Aberd.*).

Cat-hole.—1. The name given to the loop-holes or narrow openings in the wall of a barn (S.). 2. A sort of niche in the wall of a barn, in which keys and other necessaries are deposited in the inside, where it is not perforated.

Cat-hud.—The name given to a large stone, which serves as a back to a fire on the hearth in the house of a cottager (*Dumfr.*). Sw. G., *kaette*, denotes a small cell or apartment, which corresponds to the form of the country fireside; also a bed; a pen. *Hud* might seem allied to Teut. *huyd-en*, *conservare*, as the stone is meant to guard this enclosure from the effects of the fire.

Catling.—Small catgut strings for musical instruments, also a kind of knife used in surgery.

Cat-loup.—1. A very short distance as to space (S.); q. as far as a cat may leap (Hogg). 2. A moment; as, "I'se be wi' ye in a *catloup*"—*i.e.*, instantly. "I will be with you as quickly as a cat can leap."

Catmaw.—"To tumble the *catmaw*," to go topsy-turvy, to tumble (S. B.).

Catmint.—An herbaceous plant (*Mentha felina*), that cats delight to roll on.

Cat's Carriage.—The same play that is otherwise called the "King's Cushion," q.v. (*Loth.*).

Cat's Cradle.—A plaything for children, made of pack-thread on the fingers of one person, and transferred from them to those of another (*S.*).

Cat's Crammocks.—Clouds like hairs streaming from an animal's tail (*Shetland*).

Cat's Hair.—1. The down that covers unfledged birds (*Fife*); synon. *Paddockhair.* 2. The down on the face of boys before the beard grows (*S.*). 3. Applied also to the thin hair that often grows on the bodies of persons in bad health (*S.*).

Cat-siller..—The mica of mineralogists (*S.*); the *katzen silber* of the vulgar in Germany. Teut., *katten silver, amiantus, mica, vulgo argentum felium*; Kilian.

Cat's Lug.—The name given to the *Auricula ursi.*—Linn. (*Roxburgh.*).

Cat's Stairs.—A plaything for children, made of thread, small cord, or tape, which is so disposed by the hands as to fall down like steps of a stair (*Dumfr., Gall.*).

Catstone.—One of the upright stones which support a grate, there being one on each side (*Roxb.*). Since the introduction of Carron grates these *stones* are found in kitchens only. The term is said to originate from this being the favourite seat of the *cat*. *See* Catstone (English).

Catstone-head.—The flat top of the Catstone (*ibid.*).

Catsteps.—The projections of the stones in the slanting part of a gable (*Roxb.*). *Corbie-steps*, synon.

Cat's-Tails.—Hare's Tail Rush (*Eriophorum vaginatum*). Linn. *Mearns*; also called *Canna-down*, Cat Tails (*Galloway*).

Catten-Clover., Cat-in-Clover.—The Lotus (*South of S.*). Sw., *Katt-klor* (Cat's Claws).

Catter.—1. Catarrh (Bellenden). 2. A supposed disease of the fingers from handling cats.

Catterbatch.—A broil, a quarrel (*Fife*). Teut., *kater*, a he-cat, and *boetse*, rendered *cavillatio, q.*, "a cat's quarrel."

Catwittit.—Harebrained, unsettled; *q.*, having the *wits* of a *cat* (*S.*).

Kittie.—A North-country name for a cat, male or female.

Kitling.—Sharp; kitten-like.

> "His *kitling* eyes begin to runQuite through the table
> where he spiesThe horns of paperie butterflys."
>
> > *Herrick, Hesperides.*

Kittenhood.—State of being a kitten.

> "For thou art as beautiful as ever a catThat
> wantoned in the joy of kittenhood."
>
> > *Southey.*

Kittenish, kitten-like.
"Such a kittenish disposition in her, I called it; ...the love of
playfulness."—Richardson.

Kit, or *kitten.*—A young cat. A young cat is a kitten until it is
full-grown, then kittenhood ceases.

A school-boy being asked to describe a *kitten*, replied: "A *kitten*
is chiefly remarkable for rushing like mad at nothing whatever,
and generally stopping before it gets there."

Puss gentleman.—An effeminate man.—Davis, *Glossary.*

> "I cannot talk with civet in th' room,A fine
> puss gentleman that's all perfume."
>
> > *Cowper's Conversations.*

CAT PROVERBS

CAT

A BLATE cat makes a proud mouse (Scotch). An idle, or stupid, or timid foe is never feared.

A cat has nine lives, a woman has nine lives. In Middleton's *Blurt Master Constable*, 1602, we have: "They have nine lives apiece, like a woman."

A cat may look at a king. In Cornwall they say a cat may look at a king if he carries his eyes about him.

"A Cat may Look at a King," is the title of a book on history, published in the early part of the last century. On the frontispiece is the picture of a cat, over it the inscription, "A cat may look at a king," and a king's head and shoulders on the title-page, with the same inscription above.

A cat's walk, a little way and back (Cornwall). No place like home. Idling about.

A dead cat feels no cold. No life, no pain, nor reproach.

A dog hath a day.—Heywood. In Essex folks add: *And a cat has two Sundays.* Why?

The shape of a good greyhound:

218

A head like a snake, a neck like a drake,
A back like a beam, sided like a bream,

A *foot like a cat*, a tail like a rat.
Ale that would make a cat talk. Strong enough to make even the dumb speak.

"A spicy pot,
Then do's us reason,
Would make a cat
To talk high treason."

—*D'Urfey.*

A half-penny cat may look at a king (Scotch). A jeering saying of offence—"One is as good as another," and as a Scotchman once said, "and better."

A muffled cat is no good mouser.—Clarke, 1639. No good workman wears gloves. By some is said "muzzled."

A piece of a kid is worth two of a cat. A little of good is better than much that is bad.

A scalded cat fears cold water. Once bit always shy. What was may be again.

As cat or cap case.

"Bouser I am not, but mild sober Tuesday,
As catte in cap case, if I like not St. Hewsday."

The Christmas Prince, 1607.

As gray as Grannum's cat.—Hazlitt. So old as to be likely to be doubly gray.

As melancholy as a cat.—Walker. The voice of the cat is melancholy.

As melancholy as a gib-cat (Scotch). As an old, worn-out cat.—Johnston.

219

"I am as melancholy as a gib-cat or a lugged bear."[B]

Shakespeare.

Gib-cat; an old, lonely, melancholy cat.

Before the cat can lick her ear. "Nay, you were not quite out of hearing ere the cat could lick her ear."—*Oviddius Exultans*, 1673, p. 50. That is never.

Dun, besides being the name of one who arrested for debt in Henry VII.'s time, was also the name of the hangman before "Jack Ketch."—Grose.

"And presently a halter got,
Made of the best strong teer,
And ere a cat could lick her ear,
Had tied it up with so much art."

1664, Cotton's Virgile, Book 4.

By biting and scratching dogs and cats come together.— Heywood. Quarrelling oft makes friends.

Care clammed a cat.—Sir G. C. Lewis's "Herefordshire Glossary." Clammed means starvation; that is, care killed the cat; for want of food the entrails get "clammed."

Care killed the cat, but ye canna live without it. To all some trouble, though not all take heed. None know another's burden.

Care will kill a cat.

"Then hang care and sorrow,'
Tis able to kill a cat."—*D'Urfey.*

Alluding to its tenacity of life and the carking wear of care.

Cats after kind good mouse hunt.—Heywood. Letter by F. A. touching the quarrel between Arthur Hall and Melch Mallorie, in 1575-6, repr. of ed. 1580, in "Miscy. Antiq. Anglic." 1816, p. 93. "For never yet was good cat out of kinde."—*English Proverbs*, Hazlitt.

Cats and Carlins sit in the sun. When work is done then warmth and rest.

Cats eat what hussies spare. Nothing is lost. Also refers to giving away, and saying "the cat took it."

Cats hide their claws. All is not fair that seems so. Trust not to appearances.

Cry you mercy, killed my cat.—Clarke, 1639. Better away, than stay and ask pardon.

Every day's no yule; cast the cat a castock. The stump of a cabbage, and the proverb means much the same thing as "Spare no expense, bring another bottle of *small beer.*"—Denham's *Popular Sayings*, 1846.

OF FALSE PERSONS.

He bydes as fast as a cat bound with a sacer. He does as he likes; nothing holds him.

OF WITTIE PERSONS.

He can hold the cat to the sun. Bold and foolish enough for anything.

INCONSTANT PERSONS.

He is like a dog or a cat. Not reliable.

He looks like a wild cat out of a bush. Fiercely afraid.

He's like a cat; fling him which way you will, he'll not hurt. Some are always superior to misfortune, or fortune favours many.

He's like a singed cat, better than he's likely. He's better than he looks or seems.

He stands in great need that borrows the cat's dish.—Clarke,

1639. The starving are not particular. The hungry cannot choose.

He lives at the sign of the cat's foot. He is hen-pecked, his wife scratches him.—Ray.

He wald gar a man trow that the moon is made of green cheis, or the cat took the heron. Never believe all that is laid to another.

Honest as the cat when the meat is out of reach. Some are honest, but others not by choice.

How can the cat help it when the maid is a fool? Often things lost, given, or stolen, are laid to the cat.

If thou 'scap'st, thou hast cat's luck, in Fletcher's *Knight of Malta*, alluding to the activity and caution of the cat, which generally stands it in good stead.

I'll not buy a cat in a poke. F., *Chat en Poche.* See what you buy; bargain not on another's word.

Just as quick as a cat up a walnut-tree.—D'Urfey. To climb well and easily. To be alert and sudden.

Let the cat wink, and let the mouse run. For want of watching and care much is lost.—Hazlitt's "Dodsley," i. 265. The first portion is in the interlude of "The World and the Child," 1522.

Like a cat he'll fall on his legs. To succeed, never to fail, always right.

Like a cat round hot milk. Wait and have; all things come to those who wait.

Little and little the cat eateth the stickle.—Heywood. Constant dropping weareth a stone.

Long and slender like a cat's elbow.—Hazlitt. A sneer at the ill-favoured.

Love me, love my cat.—This refers to one marrying; in taking a wife he must take her belongings. Or, where you like, you must avoid contention.

Never was cat or dog drowned that could see the shore. To know the way often brings a right ending.

None but cats and dogs are allowed to quarrel here. All else agree.

No playing with a straw before an old cat.—Heywood, 1562.

Every trifling toy age cannot laugh at.—"Youth and Folly, Age and Wisdom."

Rats walk at their ease if cats do not them meese.—Wodroephe, 1623. Rogues abound where laws are weak.

Send not a cat for lard.—George Herbert. Put not any to temptation.

So as cat is after kind. Near friends are dearest. Birds of a feather flock together.

Take the chestnuts out of the fire with the cat's paw. Making use of others to save oneself.

That comes of a cat will catch mice. What is bred in the bone comes out in the flesh. Like father, like son.

The cat and dog may kiss, but are none the better friends. Policy is one thing, friendship another.

The cat invites the mouse to her feast. It is difficult for the weak to refuse the strong.

The cat is in the cream-pot. Any one's fault but hers. A row in the house (Northern).

The cat is hungry when a crust contents her. Hunger is a good sauce.

The cat is out of kind that sweet milk will not lap. One is wrong who forsakes custom.—"History of Jacob and Esau," 1568.

The cat, the rat, and Lovel the dog, rule England under one hog.—"A Myrrour for Magistrates," edition 1563, fol. 143. This couplet is a satire on Richard III. (who carried a boar on his escutcheon) and his myrmidons, *Catesby, Rat*cliffe, and Lovell.

The cat would eat fish, and would not wet her feet.—Heywood, 1562.

"Fain would the cat fish eat,But she is loth to wet her feet.""What cat's averse to fish?"—*Gray.*

Dr. Trench has pointed out the allusion to this saying in *Macbeth*, when Lady Macbeth speaks of her husband as a man,

"Letting I dare not, wait upon I would,
Like the poor cat i' the adage."

The cat sees not the mouse ever.—Heywood. Those that should hide, see more than they who seek. The fearful eye sees far.

The liquorish cat gets many a rap. The wrong-doer escapes not.

The more you rub a cat on the back, the higher she sets her tail. Praise the vain and they are more than pleased. Flattery and vanity are near akin.

The mouse lords it where the cat is not.—MS., 15th century. The little rule, where there are no great.

The old cat laps as much as the young.—Clarke. One evil is much like another.

They agree like two cats in gutter.—Heywood. To be less than friends.

They argue like cats and dogs. That is to quarrel.

Thou'lt strip it, as Stack stripped the cat when he pulled her out of the churn. To take away everything.

Though the cat winks awhile, yet sure he is not blind. To know all and pretend ignorance.

To grin like a Cheshire cat. Said to be like a cheese cat, often made in Cheshire; but this is not very clear, and the meaning doubtful.

To go like a cat on a hot bake-stone. To lose no time. To be swift and stay not.

To keep a cat from the tongs. To stop at home in idleness. It is said of a youth who stays at home with his family, when others go to the wars abroad, in "A Health to the Gentlemanly Profession of Serving Men," 1598.

Too late repents the rat when caught by the cat. Shun danger, nor dare too long.

To love it as a cat loves mustard. Not at all. To abhor.

Two cats and a mouse, two wives in one house, two dogs and one bone, never agree. No peace when all want to be masters, or to possess one object.

Well might the cat wink when both her eyes were out.

> "Sumwhat it was sayeth the proverb old,
> That the cat winked when here iye was out."

Jack Juggler, edit. 1848, p. 46.

Those bribed are worse than blind.

"*Well wots the cat whose beard she licketh.*"—Skelton's *Garlande of Laurel*, 1523.

"Wel wot nure cat whas berd he lickat."—Wright's *Essays*, vol. i. p. 149.

"The cat knoweth whose lips she licketh."—Heywood, 1562.

The first appears the most correct.

What the good wife spares the cat eats. Favourites are well cared for.

When candles are out all cats are gray. In the dark all are alike. This is said of beauty in general.

When the cat is away the mice will play.—"The Bachelor's Banquet," 1603. Heywood's "Woman Killed with Kindness," 1607. When danger is past, it is time to rejoice.

When the weasel and the cat make a marriage, it is very ill presage. When enemies counsel together, take heed; when rogues agree, let the honest folk beware.

When the maid leaves the door open, the cat's in fault. It is always well to have another to bear the blame. The way to do ill deeds oft makes ill deeds done.

Who shall hang the bell about the cat's neck?—Heywood, 1562.

> "Who shall ty the bell about the cat's necke low?
> Not I (quoth the mouse), for a thing that I know."

The mice at a consultation held how to secure themselves from the cat, resolved upon hanging a bell about her neck, to give warning when she was near; but when this was resolved, they were as far to seek; for who would do it?—R. Who will court danger to benefit others?

A Douglas in the olden time, at a meeting of conspirators, said he would "bell the cat." Afterwards the enemy was taken by him, he retaining the cognomen of "Archibald Bell-the-cat."

You can have no more of a cat than its skin. You can have no more of a man but what he can do or what he has, or no more from a jug than what it contains.

THE CAT OF SHAKESPEARE

Shakespeare mentions the cat forty-four times, and in this, like nearly all else of which he wrote, displayed both wonderful and accurate knowledge, not only of the form, nature, habits, and food of the animal, but also the inner life, the disposition, what it was, of what capable, and what it resembled. How truly he saw either from study, observation, or intuitively knew, not only the outward contour of "men and things," but could see within the casket which held the life and being, noting clearly thoughts, feelings, aspirations, intents, and purposes, not of the one only, but that also of the brute creation.

How truthfully he alludes to the peculiar eyes of the cat, the fine mark that the pupil dwindles to when the sun rides high in the heavens! Hear Grumio in *The Taming of the Shrew:*

> And so disfigure her with it, that she shall have
> no more eyes to see withal than a cat.

As to the food of the cat, he well informs us that at this distant period domestic cats were fed and cared for to a certain extent, for besides much else, he points to the fact of its love of milk in *The Tempest*, Antonio's reply to Sebastian in Act II., Scene 1:

> For all the rest,
> They'll take suggestion as a cat laps milk.

And in *King Henry the Fourth*, Act IV., Scene 2, of its pilfering ways, Falstaff cries out:

> I am as vigilant as a cat to steal cream.

While Lady Macbeth points to the uncertain, timid, cautious habits of the cat, amounting almost to cowardice:

> Letting I dare not wait upon I would,
> Like the poor cat i' the adage.

and in the same play the strange superstitious fear attached to the voice and presence of the cat at certain times and seasons:

> Thrice the brinded cat hath mewed.

The line almost carries a kind of awe with it, a sort of feeling of "what next will happen?" He noted, also, as he did most things, its marvellous powers of observation, for in *Coriolanus*, Act IV., Scene 2, occurs the following:

> Cats, that can judge as fitly.

and of the forlorn loneliness of the age-stricken male cat in *King Henry the Fourth*, Falstaff, murmuring, says:

> I am as melancholy as a gib cat.

He marks, too, the difference of action in the lion and cat, in a state of nature:

> A crouching lion and a ramping cat.

Of the night-time food-seeking cat, in *The Merchant of Venice*, old Shylock talks of the

> ...Slow in profit, and he sleeps by day
> More than the wild cat.

In the same play Shylock discourses of those that have a

natural horror of certain animals, which holds good till this day:

> Some men there are love not a gaping pig,
> Some, that are mad if they behold a cat.

and further on:

> As there is no firm reason to be rendered
> Why he cannot abide a gaping pig,
> Why he, a harmless necessary cat.

Note the distinction he makes between the wild and the domestic cat; the one, evidently, he knew the value and use of, and the other, its peculiar stealthy ways and of nature dread. In *All's Well that Ends Well*, he gives vent to his dislike; Bertram rages forth:

> I could endure anything before but a cat,
> And now he's cat to me.

The feud with the wild cat intensifies in *Midsummer Night's Dream*; 'tis Lysander speaks:

> Hang off, thou cat, thou burr, thou vile thing.

And Gremio tells of the untamableness of the wild cat, which he deems apparently impossible:

> But will you woo this wild cat?

Romeo, in *Romeo and Juliet*, looks with much disfavour, not only on cats but also dogs; in fact, the dog was held in as high disdain as the cat:

And every cat and dog,
And every little mouse, and every unworthy thing.

Here is Hamlet's opinion:

The cat will mew, the dog will have his day.

In *Cymbeline* there is:

In killing creatures vile, as cats and dogs.
The foregoing is enough to show the
great poet's opinion of the cat.

SUPERSTITION AND WITCHCRAFT

A very remarkable peculiarity of the domestic cat, and possibly one that has had much to do with the ill favour with which it has been regarded, especially in the Middle Ages, is the extraordinary property which its fur possesses of yielding electric sparks when hand-rubbed or by other friction, the black in a larger degree than any other colour, even the rapid motion of a fast retreating cat through rough, tangled underwood having been known to produce a luminous effect. In frosty weather it is the more noticeable, the coldness of the weather apparently giving intensity and brilliancy, which to the ignorant would certainly be attributed to the interference of the spiritual or superhuman. To sensitive natures and nervous temperaments the very contact with the fur of the black cat will often produce a startling thrill or absolutely an electric shock. That carefully observant naturalist, Gilbert White, speaking of the frost of 1785, notes: "During those two Siberian days my parlour cat was so electric, that had a person stroked her, and been properly insulated, the shock might have been given to a whole circle of people."

Possibly from this lively fiery sparkling tendency, combined with its noiseless motion and stealthy habits, our ancestors were led in the happily bygone superstitious days to regard the unconscious animal as a "familiar" of Satan or some other evil spirit, which generally appeared in the form of a black cat; hence witches were said to have a black cat as their "familiar," or could at will change themselves into the form of a black cat with eyes of fire. Shakespeare says, "the cat with eyne of burning coal," and in Middleton's *Witch*, Act III., Hecate says:

I will but 'noint, and then I'll mount.
(*A Spirit like a cat descends. Voice above.*)
There's one come down to fetch his dues.
(*Later on the Voice calls.*)
Hark! hark! the cat sings a brave treble in
her own language.
(*Then* Hecate.)
Now I go, now I fly,
Malkin, my sweet spirit, and I, etc.

Note.—Almost the same words are sung in the music to *Macbeth*.

"One of the frauds of witchcraft," says Timbs, "is the witch pretending to transform herself into a certain animal, the favourite and most usual transformation being a *cat*; hence cats were tormented by the ignorant vulgar."

"*Rutterkin* was a famous cat, a cat who was 'cater'-cousin to the great-great-great-great-great-great-great-great-great-grandmother of Grimalkin, and first cat in the caterie of an old woman who was tried for bewitching a daughter of the Countess of Rutland in the beginning of the sixteenth century. The monodis connects him with cats of great renown in the annals of witchcraft, a science whereto they have been allied as poor old women, one of whom, it appears, on the authority of an old pamphlet entitled 'Newes from Scotland,' etc., printed in the year 1591, 'confessed that she took a cat and christened it, etc., and that in the night following, the said cat was conveyed into the middest of the sea by all these witches sayling in their Riddles, or Cives, and so left the said cat right before the towne of Leith in Scotland. This done, there did arise such a tempest at sea as a greater hath not been seen, etc. Againe it is confessed that the said christened cat was the cause of the kinges majestie's shippe, at his coming forthe of Denmarke, had a contrarie winde to the rest of the shippes then being in his companie, which thing was most straunge and true, as the kinges majestie acknowledgeth, for when the rest of the shippes had a fair and good winde, then was the winde contrairie, and altogether against his majestie,' etc."[C]

"In some parts black cats are said to bring good luck, and in Scarborough (Henderson's 'Folk-lore of the Northern Counties'). A few years ago, sailors' wives were in the habit of keeping one, thinking thereby to ensure the safety of their husbands at sea. This, consequently, gave black cats such a value that no one else could keep them, as they were nearly always stolen. There are various proverbs which attach equal importance to this lucky animal, as, for example:

> Whenever the cat o' the house is black,
> The lasses o' lovers will have no lack.

"And again:

> Kiss the black cat,
> An' 'twill make ye fat;
> Kiss the white ane,
> 'Twill make ye lean.

"In Scotland there is a children's rhyme upon the purring of the cat:

> Dirdum drum,
> Three threads and a thrum;
> Thrum gray, thrum gray!

"In Devonshire and Wiltshire it is believed that a May cat—or, in other words, a cat born in the month of May—will never catch any rats or mice, but, contrary to the wont of cats, will bring into the house snakes, and slow-worms, and other disagreeable reptiles. In Huntingdonshire it is a common saying that 'a May kitten makes a dirty cat.' If a cat should leap over a corpse, it is said to portend misfortune. Gough, in his 'Sepulchral Monuments,' says that in Orkney, during the time the corpse remains in the house, all the cats are locked up, and the looking-glasses covered over. In Devonshire a superstition prevails that a cat will not remain in a house with an unburied corpse; and stories are often told how, on the death of one of the inmates of a house, the cat has suddenly made its disappearance, and not returned again until after the funeral. The sneezing of the cat, says Brand ('Popular Antiquities,' 1849, vol. iii., p. 187), appears to have been considered as a lucky omen to a bride who was to be married on the succeeding day.

"'In Cornwall,' says Hunt, 'those little gatherings which come on children's eyelids, locally called "whilks," and also "warts," are cured by passing the tail of a black cat nine times over the place. If a ram cat, the cure is more certain. In Ireland it is considered highly unlucky.'"[D]

Sailors are very superstitious as regards cats. If a black cat comes on board, it is a presage of disaster; if the ship's cat is more lively than ordinary, it is a sign of wind; but if the cat is accidentally drowned, then there is consternation, which does not wear off until the vessel is safe in harbour.

Lady Wilde, in her "Irish Legends," gives a cat story quite of the fairy type, and well in keeping with many of witchcraft and sorcery. "One dark, cold night, as an old woman was spinning, there came three taps at her door, and not until after the last did she open it, when a pleading voice said: 'Let me in, let me in,' and a handsome black cat, with a white breast, and two white kittens, entered. The old woman spun on, and the cats purred loudly, till the mother puss warned her that it was very late, that they wanted some milk, and that the fairies wanted her room that night to dance and sup in. The milk was given, the cats thanked her, and said they would not forget her kindness; but, ere they vanished up the chimney, they left her a great silver coin, and the fairies had their ball untroubled by the old woman's presence, for the pussy's warning was a gentle hint."

234

If a kitten comes to a house in the morning, it is lucky; if in the evening, it portends evil of some kind, unless it stays to prevent it.

A cat's hair is said to be indigestible, and if one is swallowed death will ensue (Northern).

Milton, in his "Astrologaster," p. 48, tells us: "That when the cat washes her face over her eares we shall have great store of raine."

Lord Westmoreland, in a poem "To a cat bore me company in confinement," says:

> —Scratch but thine ear,
> Then boldly tell what weather's drawing near.

The cat sneezing appears to be a lucky omen to a bride.

It was a vulgar notion that cats, when hungry, would eat coals; and even to this day, in some parts there is a doubt about it. In "The Tamer Tamed, or, Woman's Pride," Izamo says to Moroso, "I'd learn to eat coals with a hungry cat"; and in "Boduca," the first daughter says, "They are cowards; eat coals like compelled cats."

"The crying of cats, ospreys, ravens, or other birds upon the tops of houses in the night time are observed by the vulgar to presignify death to the sick."—Brand.

There is also a superstition that cats will suck the breath of infants. Nothing could be more ridiculous. The formation of the cat's mouth is not well adapted for such action, the under jaw being shorter than the upper, which is one reason why it *laps* fluids instead of drinking. Cats will creep into cradles, but for no other purpose than that of sleep, the bed and clothes being warm and soft, and of course comfortable; yet instead of doing harm, they help to keep the child's temperature more even in cold weather. Of course, if they lie on the infant, it is a different matter.

WEATHER NOTIONS

"Signs of Foul Weather," by Dr. Erasmus Darwin. In a poem, the well-known relative of the eminent Charles Darwin describes the various natural indications of coming storms. Among the animals and birds he notes the cat:

> Low o'er the grass the swallow wings;
> The cricket, too, how sharp he sings;
> Puss on the hearth, with velvet paws,
> Sits wiping o'er his whiskered jaws.

"In England," says Mr. T. F. Thiselton Dyer, "the superstitious still hold the cat in high esteem, and oftentimes, when observing the weather, attribute much importance to its various movements. Thus, according to some, when they sneeze it is a sign of rain; and Herrick, in his 'Hesperides,' tells us how:

> True calendars as pusses eare,W
> ash't o're to tell what change is neare.

"It is a common notion that when a cat scratches the legs of a table, it is a prognostic of change of weather. John Swan, in his 'Speculum Mundi' (Cambridge, 1643), writing of the cat, says: 'She useth therefore to wash her face with her feet, which she licketh and moisteneth with her tongue; and it is observed by some that if she put her feet beyond the crown of her head in this kind of washing, it is a signe of rain.' Indeed, in the eyes of the superstitious, there is scarcely a movement of the cat which is not supposed to have some significance.

"Cats are exceedingly fond of valerian (*V. officinalis*), and in

236

Topsell's 'Four-footed Beasts' (1658, p. 81), we find the following curious remarks: 'The root of the herb valerian (called *Phu*), is very like to the eye of a cat, and wheresoever it groweth, if cats come thereunto, they instantly dig it up for the love thereof, as I myself have seen in mine own garden, for it smelleth moreover like a cat.' There is also an English rhyme on the plant *marum* to the following effect:

> If you see it,
> The cats will eat it;
> If you sow it,
> The cats will know it.

"In Suffolk, cats' eyes are supposed to dilate and contract with the flow and ebb of the tide. In Lancashire the common people have an idea that those who play much with cats never have good health."[E]

If tincture of valerian is sprinkled on a plant or bush the neighbouring cats roll and rub themselves on or against it, often biting and scratching the plant to pieces.—H. W.

In Lancashire it is regarded as unlucky to allow a cat to die in a house. Hence,[F] when they are ill they are usually drowned.

At Christ Church, Spitalfields, there is a benefaction for the widows of weavers under certain restrictions, called "cat and dog money." There is a tradition in the parish that money was given in the first instance to cats and dogs.[G]

If a cat tears at the cushions, carpet, and other articles of furniture with its claws, it is considered a sign of wind. Hence the saying, "the cat is raising the wind."

Mr. Park's note in his copy of Bourn and Brand's "Popular Antiquities," p. 92, says: "Cats sitting with their tails to the fire, or washing with their paws behind their ears, are said to foretell a change of weather."

In Pules' play of "The Novice" is the line:

Ere Gil, our cat, can lick her ear.

This is from Brand, and I do not think it refers to the weather, but to an impossibility.

A CAT-CLOCK

The following curious incident is to be found in Huc's "Chinese Empire":

"One day, when we went to pay a visit to some families of Chinese Christian peasants, we met, near a farm, a young lad, who was taking a buffalo to graze along our path. We asked him carelessly as we passed whether it was yet noon. The child raised his head to look at the sun, but it was hidden behind thick clouds, and he could read no answer there. 'The sky is so cloudy,' said he; 'but wait a moment;' and with these words he ran towards the farm, and came back a few minutes afterwards with a cat in his arms. 'Look here,' said he, 'it is not noon yet;' and he showed us the cat's eyes by pushing up the lids with his hands. We looked at the child with surprise; but he was evidently in earnest, and the cat, though astonished, and not much pleased at the experiment made on her eyes, behaved with most exemplary complaisance. 'Very well,' said we, 'thank you;' and he then let go the cat, who made her escape pretty quickly, and we continued our route. To say the truth, we had not at all understood the proceeding, but did not wish to question the little pagan, lest he should find out that we were Europeans by our ignorance. As soon as we reached the farm, however, we made haste to ask our Christians whether they could tell the clock by looking into the cat's eyes. They seemed surprised at the question, but as there was no danger in confessing to them our ignorance of the properties of the cat's eyes, we related what had just taken place. That was all that was necessary; our complaisant neophytes immediately gave chase to all the cats in the neighbourhood. They brought us three or four, and explained in what manner they might be made use of for watches. They pointed out that the pupils of their eyes went on constantly growing narrower until twelve o'clock, when they became like a fine line, as thin as a hair, drawn perpendicularly across the eye, and that after twelve the dilatation recommenced."

* * * * *

"Archbishop Whately once declared that there was only one noun in English which had a real vocative case. It was 'cat,' vocative 'puss.' I wonder if this derivation is true (I take it from a New York journal): When the Egyptians of old worshipped the cat they settled it that she was like the moon, because she was more bright at night, and because her eyes changed just as the moon changes—from new, to crescent, and to full. So they made an idol of the cat's head, and named it *pasht*, which meant the face of the moon. *Pasht* became pas, pus, puss."—*Church Times*, March 8th, 1888.

"PUSS IN BOOTS"
(LE CHAT BOTTÉ)

Is from the "Eleventh Night" of Straparola's Italian fairy tales, where Constantine's cat procures his master a fine castle and the king's heiress, first translated into French in 1585. Our version is taken from that of Charles Perrault. There is a similar one in the Scandinavian nursery tales. This clever cat secures a fortune and a royal partner for his master, who passes off as the Marquis of Carabas, but is in reality a young miller, without a penny in the world.

The above is from Dr. Brewer's "Dictionary of Phrase and Fable," and goes far to prove the antiquity of what is generally believed to be a modern story, many believing it to be one of the numberless pleasant, amusing, and in a sense instructive nursery or children's stories of the present time.

SIGNS

D'Urfey, in his poem on Knole, speaks of "The Cats" at Sevenoaks.

"The Cat" or "Cats" is by no means a common sign. The subject is well alluded to in "The Cat, Past and Present," from the French of M. Champfleury, translated by Mrs. Cashel Hoey, at page 33. A sign is pictured from the Lombards' quarter, Paris. It is there over a confectioner's shop, and is a cat seated, or rather two, a sign being placed on either side of the corner. Underneath one is "Au Chat," the other, "Noir." I may add the work is a most excellent and amusing collection of much appertaining to cats, and is well worthy of a place in the cat-lover's library.

In Larwood and Hotten's "History of Sign-boards," a work of much research and merit, occurs the following: "As I was going through a street of London where I had never been till then, I felt a general damp and faintness all over me which I could not tell how to account for, till I chanced to cast my eyes upwards, and found I was passing under a sign-post on which the picture of a *cat* was hung." This little incident of the cat-hater, told in No. 538 of *The Spectator*, is a proof of the presence of cats on the sign-board, where, indeed, they are still to be met with, but very rarely. There is a sign of "The Cat" at Egremont, in Cumberland, a "Black Cat" at St. Leonard's Gate, Lancaster, and a "Red Cat" at Birkenhead; and a "Red Cat" in the Hague, Holland, to which is attached an amusing story worthy of perusal.

"The Cat and Parrot" and "The Cat and Lion" apparently have no direct meaning, unless by the former may be inferred that if you lap like a cat of the liquids sold at the hostelry, you will talk like a parrot; yet, according to Larwood and Hotten, it was a bookseller's sign.

"The Cat and Cage" and "The Cat in Basket" were signs much in vogue during the frost fair on the Thames in 1739-40, a live cat being hung outside some of the booths, which afterwards was not infrequent at other festive meetings. What the exact origin was is not quite apparent.

"'Cat and Fiddle,' a public-house sign, is a corruption either of the French *Catherine la fidèle*, wife of Czar Peter the Great of Russia, or of *Caton le fidèle*, meaning Caton, governor of Calais."—Dr. Brewer's *Dictionary of Phrase and Fable*.

Cat and Fiddle.—"While on the subject of sign-boards," says a writer in Cassell's "Old and New London," vol. i., p. 507, "we may state that Piccadilly was the place in which 'The Cat and Fiddle' first appeared as a public-house sign. The story is that a Frenchwoman, a small shopkeeper at the eastern end soon after it was built, had a very faithful and favourite cat, and that in the lack of any other sign she put over her door the words, 'Voici un Chat fidèle.' From some cause or other the 'Chat fidèle' soon became a popular sign in France, and was speedily Anglicised into 'The Cat and Fiddle,' because the words form part of one of our most popular nursery rhymes. We do not pledge ourselves as to the accuracy of this definition."

"In Farringdon (Devon) is the sign of 'La Chatte Fidèle,' in commemoration of a faithful cat. Without scanning the phrase too nicely, it may simply indicate that the game of *cat* (trap-ball) and a *fiddle* for dancing are provided for customers."

Yet, according to Larwood and Hotten's "History of Sign-boards," there is yet another version, and another, of the matter, for it is stated, "a little hidden meaning is there in the 'Cat and Fiddle,' still a great favourite in Hampshire, the only connection between the animal and the instrument being that the strings are made from cats' entrails (*sic*), and that a small fiddle is called a *kit*, and a small cat a *kitten*; besides, they have been united from time immemorial in the nursery rhyme:

Heigh diddle diddle,
The Cat and the fiddle."

Amongst the other explanations offered is the one that it may have originated with the sign of a certain *Caton Fidèle*, a staunch Protestant in the reign of Queen Mary, and only have been changed into the cat and fiddle by corruption; but if so it must have lost its original appellation very soon, for as early as 1589 we find "Henry Carr, signe of the *Catte and Fidle* in the olde Chaunge." Formerly there was a "*Cat and Fiddle* at Norwich, the Cat being represented playing on a fiddle, and a number of mice dancing round her."

Cat and Bagpipes.—Was not uncommon in Ireland, this instrument being the national one in place of the fiddle.

When doctors disagree, who shall decide? Thus I leave it.

Cat and Mutton, from Cassell's "Old and New London," vol. iv., p. 223:

"Near the Imperial Gas Works, Haggerston, is Goldsmith's row; this was formerly known as Mutton Lane, a name still given to that part of the thoroughfare bordering on the southern extremity of London Fields, where stands a noted public-house rejoicing in the sign of the 'Cat and Mutton' affixed to the house, and *two* sign-boards, which are rather curious. They have upon them the following doggerel lines:

Pray Puss do not tare,
Because the Mutton is so rare.
Pray Puss do not claw,
Because the Mutton is so raw.

Cat and Wheel.—Most likely to be a corruption of Catherine Wheel; there was a sign of this name in the Borough, Southwark.

In France some signs are still more peculiar, as a "Cat Playing at Raquet" (*Chatte qui pelote*), "Fishing Cat" (*La Chatte qui pêche*), "The Dancing Cat," and the well-known "Puss in Boots."

"Whittington and his Cat" is by no means uncommon, and was not unknown in the early part of the seventeenth century. Somewhere I remember having seen "Whittington's Cat" without the master, which, I suppose, arose from the painter not knowing how to portray "Sir Richard."

"*Cat and Kittens.*—A public-house sign, alluding to the pewter pots so called. Stealing these pots is termed 'Cat and kitten sneaking.' We still call a large kettle a *kitchen*, and speak of a soldier's *kit* (Saxon, *cytel*, a pot, pan, or vessel generally)."— Brewer's *Dictionary of Phrase and Fable*.

May not this sign be intended to mean merely what is shown, "The Cat and Kittens," indicative of comfort and rest? Or may it have been "Cat and *Chitterlings*," in allusion to the source from which fiddlestrings were said to be derived?

Cat and Tortoise.—This seems to have no meaning other than at a tavern extremes meet, the fast and the slow, the lively and the stolid; or it is possibly a corruption of something widely different.

THE LAW ON CAT KILLING

An "Articled Clerk," writing to *The Standard* with regard to the illegality of killing cats, states: "It is clearly laid down in 'Addison on Torts,' that a person is not justified in killing his neighbour's cat, or dog, which he finds on his land, unless the animal is in the act of doing some injurious act which can only be prevented by its slaughter.

"And it has been decided by the case of 'Townsend v. Watken' 9 last 277, that if a person sets on his lands a trap for foxes, and baits it with such strong-smelling meat as to attract his neighbour's dog or cat on to his land, to the trap, and such animal is thereby killed or injured, he is liable for the act, though he had no intention of doing it, and though the animal ought not to have been on his land."

DEAD CATS

Lifeless cats have been from time immemorial suggestive of foolish hoaxing, a parcel being made up, or a basket with the legs of a hare projecting, directed to some one at a distance, and on which the charge for carriage comes to a considerable sum, the *fortunate* recipient ultimately, to his great annoyance, finding "his present" was nothing else but "a dead cat." Dead cats, which not infrequently were cast into the streets, or accidentally killed there, were sometimes used as objects of sport by the silly, low-minded, and vulgar, and it was thought a "clever thing" if they could deposit such in a drawing-room through an open window, or pitch the unfortunate animal, often crushed and dirty, into a passing carriage; but "the time of times" when it was considered to be a legitimate object to use was that of either a borough or county election, cats and rotten eggs forming the material with which the assault was conducted in the event of an unpopular candidate for honours attempting to give his political views to a depreciatory mob surrounding the hustings. An anecdote is recorded in Grose's "Olio" of Mr. Fox, who, in 1784, was a candidate for Westminster, which goes far to show what dirty, degrading, disgusting indignities the would-be "*people's* representative" had to endure at that period, and with what good humour such favours of popular appreciation, or otherwise, were received:

"During the poll, a dead cat being thrown on the hustings, one of Sir Cecil Wray's party observed it stunk worse than *a fox*; to which Mr. Fox replied there was nothing extraordinary in that, considering it was a 'poll cat.'"

This is by no means the only ready and witty answer that has been attributed to Mr. Fox, though not bearing on the present subject.

THE CAT AS A TORMENTOR

Shakespeare, in "Lucrece," says:

"Yet foul night-waking cat, he doth but dally,
While in his holdfast foot the weak mouse panteth."

In an essay on "The Art of Ingeniously Tormenting" (1753), the cat is alluded to in the frontispiece—a cat at play with a mouse, below which is the couplet:

The cat doth play,
And after slay.

Child's Guide.

Giovanni Batista Casti, in his book, "Tre Giuli" (1762), likens the cat to one who lends money, and suddenly pounces on the debtor:

Thus sometimes with a mouse, ere nip,
The cat will on her hapless victim smile,
Until at length she gives the fatal grip.

Again, John Philips, in the latter part of the seventeenth century, in his poem of "The Splendid Shilling," referring to debtors, writes:

Grimalkin to Domestick Vermin sworn
An everlasting Foe, with watchful Eye
Lies nightly brooding o'er a chinky Gap
Protending her fell Claws, to thoughtless MiceSure Ruin.

249

HERALDRY, ETC

A cat (hieroglyphically) represents false friendship, or a deceitful, flattering friend.

The cat (in heraldry) is an emblem of liberty, because it naturally dislikes to be shut up, and therefore the Burgundians, etc., bore a cat on their banners to intimate they could not endure servitude.

"It is a bold and daring creature and also cruel to its enemy, and never gives over till it has destroyed it, if possible. It is also watchful, dexterous, swift, pliable, and has good nerves—thus, if it falls from a place never so high, it still alights on its feet; and therefore may denote those who have much forethought, that whatsoever befalls them they are still on their guard."

"In coat armour they must always be represented as full-faced, and not showing one side of it, but both their eyes and both their ears. *Argent* three cats in pale *sable* is the coat of the family of Keat of Devonshire."

Many families have adopted the cat as their emblem. In "Cats, Past and Present," several are noted. In Scotland, the Clan Chattan bore as their chief cognizance the wild cat, and called their chief "Mohr au Chat," the great wild cat. Nor is the name uncommon as an English surname, frequently appearing as Cat, Catt, Catte; but the most strange association of the name with the calling was one I knew in my old sporting days of a *gamekeeper* whose name was Cat.

PERFORMING CATS

Cats, unlike dogs, are not amused by, nor do they in any way take an interest in what are termed "tricks." Performing dogs will sit about their master watching anxiously for their turn, and they have been known on more than one occasion to slip before the dog that has next jump through the hoop or over a stick, barking merrily, exulting in having excelled the other; generally they await with intense eagerness the agility of the others and strenuously try to surpass them. Possibly this is so from the long time the dog has been under the dominion of man, and *taught* by him how to be of service, either in *hunting, sporting, shepherding, watching*; in a sense his friend, though more his bond or slave, even to dragging carts, waggons, and sleighs, to fetch and carry, even to smuggle. *Long teaching, persistent teaching from time immemorial* has undoubtedly had its due effect, and in some instances, if not all, has been *transmitted*, such as in the pointer and setter, which particular sections have been known to require little or no present training, taking to their duties naturally, receiving but little guidance as to how much, when, and where such instinctive qualities are required.

With the cat it is widely different. Beyond being the "necessary" cat, the pet cat or kitten, it never has been an object of interest, beyond that of keeping from increase those veritable plagues, rats and mice; the enormous use it has thus been to man has had but scant acknowledgment, never thoroughly appreciated, vastly underrated, with but little attention not only to its beauty, nor in modifying its nature to the actual *requirements* of civilisation. The cat through long ages has had, as it were, to shift for itself; with the *few* approved, with the *many* not only neglected, but in bygone days, and with some even in the present, it has been, and is looked on as a thing that is not to be cared for, or domesticated, but often absolutely ill-treated, not because there has been wrong done, but because it is *a cat*. I heard a man of "gentle blood" once say that there was no good in a cat, and the only use they were, as far as *he* could see, was as an animal to try the courage of his terriers upon.

Happily all are not alike, and so the cat survives, and by the present generation is petted and noticed with a growing interest. Though long closely connected with man in many ways, still, as I have before said, it has been left to itself to a certain degree. In no way, or but slightly, has it been guided; and thus, as a domestic animal, it has become what it is—one repelling most attempts to make it of the same kind of value as the dog; its great powers of observation, coupled with timidity, make a barrier to its being trained into that which its nature dislikes; and its natural and acquired repugnance to confinement and tuition prevent it—at least at present—from being "the humble servant," as the dog, "past and present," has been and is.

Studying closely the habits of the cat for years, as I have, I believe there is a natural sullen antipathy to being taught or restrained, or *made* to do anything to which its nature or feelings are averse; and this arises from long-continued persecution and no training. Try, for instance, to make a cat lie still if it wants to go out. You may hold it at first, then gently relinquish your grasp, stroke it, talk to it, fondle it, until it purrs, and purrs with seeming pleasure, but it *never once forgets it is restrained*, and *the first* opportunity it will make a sudden dash, and is—gone.

However, all animals, more or less, may be trained, and the cat, of course, is among them, and a notable one. By bringing them up among birds, such as canaries, pigeons, chickens, and ducklings, it will respect and not touch them, while those wild will be immediately sacrificed.

One of the best instances of this was a small collection of animals and birds in a large cage that used to be shown by a man by the name of Austin, and to which I have already referred. This man was a lover and trainer of animal life, and an adept. His "Happy Family" generally consisted of a cat or two, some kittens, rats, mice, rabbits, guinea pigs, an owl, a kestrel falcon, starlings, goldfinches, canaries, etc.—a most incongruous assembly. Yet among them all there was a *freedom of action*, a self-reliance, and an air of happiness that I have never seen in "performing cats." Mr. Austin informed me that he had been a number of years studying their different natures, but that he found the cats the most difficult to deal with, only the most gentle treatment accomplishing the object he had in view. Any fresh introduction had to be done by degrees, and shown outside first for some time. It was quite apparent, however, that the cats were *quite at their ease*, and I have seen a canary sitting on the head of the cat, while a starling was resting on the back. But all are gone—Austin and his pets—and no other reigns in his stead.

Occasionally one sees, at the corners of some of the London streets, a man who professes to have *trained* cats and birds; the latter, certainly, are clever, but the former have a frightened, scared look, and seem by no means comfortable. I should say the tuition was on different lines to that of Austin. The man takes a canary, opens a cat's mouth, puts it in, takes it out, *makes* the cat, or cats, go up a short ladder and down another; then they are *told* to fight, and placed in front of each other; but fight they will not with their fore-paws, so the *master* moves their paws for them, *each looking away* from the other. There is no training in this but *fear*. There is an innate timidity, the offspring of long persecution, in the cat that prevents, as a rule, its performing in public. Not so the dog; time and place matter not to him; from generation to generation he *has been used to it*.

In "Cats Past and Present," by Champfleury, there are descriptions of performing cats, and one Valmont de Bomare mentions that in a booth at the fair of St. Germain's, during the eighteenth century, there was a cat concert, the word "Miaulique," in huge letters, being on the outside. In 1789 there is an account of a Venetian giving cat concerts, and the facsimile of a print of the seventeenth century picturing a cat showman.

"In 1758, or the following year, Bisset, the famous animal trainer, hired a room near the Haymarket, at which he announced a public performance of a 'Cats' Opera,' supplemented by tricks of a horse, a dog, and some monkeys, etc. The 'Cats' Opera' was attended by crowded houses, and Bisset cleared a thousand pounds in a few days. After a successful season in London, he sold some of the animals, and made a provincial tour with the rest, rapidly accumulating a considerable fortune."—Mr. Frost's *Old Showman.*

"Many years ago a concert was given at Paris, wherein cats were the performers. They were placed in rows, and a monkey beat time to them. According as he beat the time so the cats mewed; and the historian of the fact relates that the diversity of the tones which they emitted produced a very ludicrous effect. This exhibition was announced to the Parisian public by the title of *Concert Miaulant.*"—*Zoological Anecdotes.*

Another specimen of *discipline* is to be found in "Menageries." The writer says: "Cats may be taught to perform tricks, such as leaping over a stick, but they always do such feats unwillingly. There is at present an exhibition of cats in Regent Street, who, at the bidding of their master, an Italian, turn a wheel and draw up water in a bucket, ring a bell; and in doing these things begin, continue, and stop as they are commanded. But the *commencez, continuez, arrêtez* of their keeper is always enforced with a threatening eye, and often with a severe blow; and the poor creatures exhibit the greatest reluctance to proceed with their unnatural employments. They have a subdued and piteous look; but the scratches upon their master's arms show that *his* task is not always an easy one."

Of performing cats on the stage, there have been several "companies" of late in London, one of which I went to see at the royal Aquarium, Westminster; and I am bound to say that the relations between master and cats were on a better footing than any that have hitherto come under my notice. On each side of the stage there were cat kennels, from which the cats made their appearance on a given signal, ran across, on or over whatever was placed between, and disappeared quickly into the opposite kennels. But about it all there was a decided air of *timidity*, and an eagerness to *get the performance over*, and *done with it*. When the cats came out they were caressed and encouraged, which seemed to have a soothing effect, and I have a strong apprehension that they received some dainty morsel when they reached their destination. One ran up a pole at command, over which there was a cap at the top, into which it disappeared for a few seconds, evidently for some reason, food *perhaps*. It then descended. But before this supreme act several cats had crossed a bridge of chairs, stepping only on the backs, until they reached the opposite house or box into which to retire. The process was repeated, and the performance varied by two cats crossing the bridge together, one passing over and the other under the horizontal rung between the seat and the top of the chair. A long plank was next produced, upon which was placed a row of wine-bottles at intervals; and the cats ran along the plank, winding in and out between the bottles, first to the right, then to the left, without making a mistake. This part of the performance was varied by placing on the top of each bottle a flat disc of thick wood; one of the cats strode then from disc to disc, without displacing or upsetting a bottle, while the other animal repeated its serpentine walk on the plank below. The plank being removed, a number of trestles were brought in, and placed at intervals in a row between the two sets of houses, when the cats, on being called, jumped from trestle to trestle, varying the feat by leaping through a hoop, which was held up by the trainer between the trestles. To this succeeded a performance on the tight rope, which was not the least curious part of the exhibition. A rope being stretched across the arena from house to house, the cats walked across in turn, without making a mistake. Some white rats were then brought and placed at intervals along the rope, when the cats, re-crossing from one end to the other, strode over the rats without injuring them. A repetition of this feat was rendered a little more difficult by substituting for rats, which sat pretty quietly in one place, several white mice and small birds, which were more restless, and kept changing their positions. The cats re-crossed the rope, and passed over all these obstacles without even noticing the impediments placed in their way, with one or two exceptions, when they stopped, and cosseted one or more of the white rats, two of which rode triumphantly on the back of a large black cat.

Perhaps the most odd performance was that of "Cat Harris," an imitator of the voice of cats in 1747.

"When Foote first opened the Haymarket Theatre, amongst other projects he proposed to entertain the public with imitation of cat-music. For this purpose he engaged a man famous for his skill in mimicking the mewing of the cat. This person was called 'Cat Harris.' As he did not attend the rehearsal of this odd concert, Foote desired Shuter would endeavour to find him out and bring him with him. Shuter was directed to some court in the Minories, where this extraordinary musician lived; but, not being able to find the house, Shuter began a cat solo; upon this the other looked out of the window, and answered him with a cantata of the same sort. 'Come along,' said Shuter; 'I want no better information that you are the man. Foote stays for us; we cannot begin the cat-opera without you.'"—Cassell's *Old and New London*, vol. iv.

CAT-RACING IN BELGIUM

"On festival days, parties of young men assemble in various places to shoot with cross-bows and muskets, and prizes of considerable value are often distributed to the winners. Then there are pigeon-clubs and canary-clubs, for granting rewards to the trainers of the fleetest carrier-pigeons and best warbling canaries. Of these clubs many individuals of high rank are the honorary presidents, and even royal princes deign to present them banners, without which no Belgian club can lay claim to any degree of importance." But the most curious thing is cat-racing, which takes place, according to an engraving, in the public thoroughfare, the cats being turned loose at a given time. It is thus described: "Cat-racing is a sport which stands high in popular favour. In one of the suburbs of Liège it is an affair of annual observance during carnival time. Numerous individuals of the feline tribe are collected, each having round his neck a collar with a seal attached to it, precisely like those of the carrier-pigeons. The cats are tied up in sacks, and as soon as the clock strikes the solemn hour of midnight the sacks are unfastened, the cats let loose, and the race begins. The winner is the cat which first reaches home, and the prize awarded to its owner is sometimes a ham, sometimes a silver spoon. On the occasion of the last competition the prize was won by a blind cat."—*Pictorial Times*, June 16th, 1860.

CAT IMAGES

Those with long memories will not have forgotten the Italian with a board on his head, on which were tied a number of plaster casts, and possibly still seem to hear, in the far away time, the unforgotten cry of "Yah im-a-gees." Notably, among these works of art, were models of cats—such cats, such expressive faces; and what forms! How droll, too, were those with a moving head, wagging and nodding, as it were, with a grave and thoughtful, semi-reproachful, vacant gaze! "Yah im-a-gees" has passed on, and the country pedlar, with his "crockery" cats, mostly red and white. "Sure such cats alive were never seen?" but in burnt clay they existed, and often *adorned* the mantel-shelves of the poor. What must the live cat sitting before the fire have thought—if cats think—when it looked up at the stolid, staring, stiff and stark new-comer? One never sees these things now; nor the cats made of paste-board covered with black velvet, and two large brass spangles for eyes. These were put into dark corners with an idea of deception, with the imbecile hope that visitors would take them to be real flesh and bone everyday black cats. But was any one ever taken in but—the maker? Then there were cats, and cats and kittens, made of silk, for selling at fancy fairs, not much like cats, but for the *purposes* good. Cats sitting on pen-wipers; clay cats of burnt brick-earth. These were generally something to remember rather than possess. Wax cats also, with a cotton wick coming out at the top of the head. It was a saddening sight to see these *beauties* burning slowly away. Was this a "remnant" of the burning of the live cats in the "good old times?" And cats made of rabbits' skins were not uncommon, and far better to give children to play with than the tiny, lovable, patient, live kitten, which, if it submit to be tortured, it is well, but if it resent pain and suffering, then it is beaten. There is more ill done "from want of thought than want of heart."

But kittens have fallen upon evil times, ay, even in these days of education and enlightenment. As long as the world lasts probably there will be the foolish, the gay, unthinking, and, in tastes, the ridiculous. But then there are, and there ever will be, those that are always craving, thirsting, longing, shall I say *mad*?—for something *new*. Light-headed, with softened intellects who must—*they* say *they must*—have some excitement or some novelty, no matter what, to talk of or possess, though all this is ephemeral, and the silliness only lasts a few hours. Long or short, they are never conscious of these absurdities, and look forward with all the eagerness of doll-pleased infancy for another—craze. The world is being denuded of some of its brightest ornaments and its heaven-taught music, in the slaughter of birds, to gratify for scarcely a few hours the insane vanity, that is now rife in the ball-room—fashion.

What has all this to do with cats? Why, this class of people are not content, they never are so; but are adding to the evil by piling up a fresh one. It is the kitten now, the small, about two or three weeks old kitten that is the "fashion." Not long ago they were killed and stuffed for children to play with—better so than alive, perhaps; but now they are to please children of a larger *growth*, their tightly filled skins, adorned with glass eyes, being put in sportive attitudes about portrait frames, and such like uses. It is comical, and were it not for the stupid bad taste and absurdity of the thing, one would feel inclined to laugh at *clambering* kitten skins about, and supposed to be peeping into the face of a languor-struck "beauty." Who buys such? Does any one? If so, where do they go? Over thirty kittens in one shop window. What next, and—next? Truly frivolity is not dead!

From these, and such as these, turn to the models fair and proper; the china, the porcelain, the terra cotta, the bronze, and the silver, both English, French, German, and Japanese; some exquisite, with all the character, elegance, and grace of the living animals. In these there has been a great advance of late years, Miss A. Chaplin taking the lead. Then in bold point tracery on pottery Miss Barlow tells of the animal's flowing lines and non-angular posing. Art—true art—all of it; and art to be coveted by the lover of cats, or for art alone.

But I have almost forgotten the old-time custom of, when the young ladies came from school, bringing home a "sampler," in the days before linen stamping was known or thought of. On these in needlework were alphabets, numbers, trees (such trees), dogs, and cats. Then, too, there were cats of silk and satin, in needlework, and cats in various materials; but the most curious among the young people's accomplishments was the making of tortoiseshell cats from a snail-shell, with a smaller one for a head, with either wax or bread ears, fore-legs and tail, and yellow or green beads for eyes. Droll-looking things—very. I give a drawing of one. And last, not least often, the edible cats— cats made of cheese, cats of sweet sponge-cake, cats of sugar, and once I saw a cat of jelly. In the old times of country pleasure fairs, when every one brought home gingerbread nuts and cakes as "a fairing," the gingerbread "cat in boots" was not forgotten nor left unappreciated; generally fairly good in form, and gilt over with Dutch metal, it occupied a place of honour in many a country cottage home, and, for the matter of that, also in the busy town. If good gingerbread, it was saved for many a day, or until the holiday time was ended and feasting over, and the next fair talked of.

But, after all "said and done," what a little respect, regard, and reverence is there in our mode to that of the Egyptians! They had three varieties of cats, but they were all the same to them; as their pets, as useful, beautiful, and typical, they were individually and nationally regarded, their bodies embalmed, and verses chaunted in their praise; and the image of the cat then—a thousand years ago—was a deity. What do they think of the cat now, these same though modern Egyptians? Scarcely anything. And we, who in bygone ages persecuted it, to-day give it a growing recognition as an animal both useful, beautiful, and worthy of culture.

LOVERS OF CATS

"The Turks greatly admire Cats; to them, their alluring Figure appears preferable to the Docility, Instinct, and Fidelity of the Dog. Mahomet was very partial to Cats. It is related, that being called up on some urgent Business, he preferred *cutting off* the Sleeve of his Robe, to *waking* the Cat, that lay upon it *asleep*. Nothing more was necessary, to bring these Animals into high Request. A Cat may even enter a Mosque; it is caressed there, as the Favourite Animal of the Prophet; while the Dog, that should dare appear in the Temples, would *pollute* them with his Presence, and would be punished with instant *Death*."[H]

I am indebted to the Rev. T. G. Gardner, of St. Paul's Cray, for the following from the French:

"A recluse, in the time of Gregory the Great, had it revealed to him in a vision that in the world to come he should have equal share of beatitude with that Pontiff; but this scarcely contented him, and he thought some compensation was his due, inasmuch as the Pope enjoyed immense wealth in this present life, and he himself had nothing he could call his own save one pet cat. But in another vision he was censured; his worldly detachment was not so entire as he imagined, and that Gregory would with far greater equanimity part with his vast treasures than he could part with his beloved puss."

Cats Endowed by La Belle Stewart.—One of the chief ornaments of the Court of St. James', in the reign of Charles II., was "La Belle Stewart," afterwards the Duchess of Richmond, to whom Pope alluded as the "Duchess of R." in the well-known line:

Die and endow a college or a cat.

The endowment satirised by Pope has been favourably explained by Warton. She left annuities to several female friends, with the burden of maintaining some of her cats—a delicate way of providing for poor and probably proud gentlewomen, without making them feel that they owed their livelihood to her mere liberality. But possibly there may have been a kindliness of thought for both, deeming that those who were dear friends would be most likely to attend to her wishes.

Mr. Samuel Pepys had at least a gentle nature as regards animals, if he was not a lover of cats, for in his Diary occurs this note as to the Fire of London, 1666:

"*September 5th.*—Thence homeward having passed through Cheapside and Newgate Market, all burned; and seen Antony Joyce's house on fire. And took up (which I keep by me) a piece of glass of Mercer's chapel in the street, where much more was, so melted and buckled with the heat of the fire like parchment. I did also see a poor cat taken out of a hole in a chimney, joining the wall of the Exchange, with the hair all burned off its body and yet alive."

Dr. Jortin wrote a Latin epitaph on a favourite cat:[1]

IMITATED IN ENGLISH.

"Worn out with age and dire disease, a cat, Friendly to all, save wicked mouse and rat, I'm sent at last to ford the Stygian lake, And to the infernal coast a voyage make. Me *Proserpine* receiv'd, and smiling said, 'Be bless'd within these mansions of the dead. Enjoy among thy velvet-footed loves, Elysian's sunny banks and shady groves.' 'But if I've well deserv'd (O gracious queen), If patient under sufferings I have been, Grant me at least one night to visit home again, Once more to see my home and mistress dear, And purr these grateful accents in her ear: "Thy faithful cat, thy poor departed slave, Still loves her mistress, e'en beyond the grave.""

"Dr. Barker kept a Seraglio and Colony of Cats. It happened, that at the Coronation of George I. the Chair of State fell to his Share of the Spoil (as Prebendary of Westminster) which he sold to some Foreigner; when they packed it up, one of his favourite Cats was inclosed along with it; but the Doctor pursued his treasure in a boat to Gravesend and recovered her safe. When the Doctor was disgusted with the *Ministry*, he gave his *Female* Cats, the Names of the *Chief Ladies* about the Court; and the *Male-ones*, those of the *Men in Power*, adorning them with the Blue, Red, or Green Insignia of Ribbons, which the Persons they represented, wore."[J]

Daniel, in his "Rural Sports," 1813, mentions the fact that, "In one of the Ships of the Fleet, that sailed lately from Falmouth, for the West Indies, went as Passengers a Lady and her *seven Lap-dogs*, for the Passage of *each* of which, she paid *Thirty Pounds*, on the express Condition, that they were to *dine* at the Cabin-table, and lap their *Wine* afterwards. Yet these happy dogs do not engross the *whole* of their good Lady's Affection; she has also, in Jamaica, Forty Cats, and a Husband."

"The Partiality to the *domestic* Cat, has been thus established. Some Years since, a Lady of the name of Greggs, died at an advanced Age, in Southampton Row, London. Her fortune was *Thirty Thousand Pounds*, at the Time of her Decease. *Credite Posteri!* her *Executors* found in her House *Eighty-six living*, and *Twenty-eight dead Cats*. Her Mode of Interring them, was, as they died, to place them in different Boxes, which were heaped on one another in Closets, as the *Dead* are described by Pennant, to be in the Church of St. Giles. She had a black Female Servant— to Her she left One hundred and fifty pounds *per annum* to keep the *Favourites*, whom she left *alive*."[K]

The Chantrel family of Rottingdean seem also to be possessed with a similar kind of feeling towards cats, exhibiting no fewer than twenty-one specimens at one Cat Show, which at the time were said to represent only a small portion of their stock; these ultimately became almost too numerous, getting beyond control.

Signor Foli is a lover of cats, and has exhibited at the Crystal Palace Cat Show.

Petrarch loved his cat almost as much as he loved Laura, and when it died he had it embalmed.

Tasso addressed one of his best sonnets to his female cat.

Cardinal Wolsey had his cat placed near him on a chair while acting in his judicial capacity.

Sir I. Newton was also a lover of cats, and there is a good story told of the philosopher having two holes made in a door for his cat and her kitten to enter by—a *large* one for the cat, and a *small* one for the kitten.

Peg Woffington came to London at twenty-two years of age. After calling many times unsuccessfully at the house of John Rich, the manager of Covent Garden, she at last sent up her name. She was admitted, and found him lolling on a sofa, surrounded by twenty-seven cats of all ages.

The following is from the *Echo*, respecting a lady well known in her profession: "Miss Ellen Terry has a passionate fondness for cats. She will frolic for hours with her feline pets, never tiring of studying their graceful gambols. An author friend of mine told me of once reading a play to her. During the reading she posed on an immense tiger-skin, surrounded by a small army of cats. At first the playful capers of the mistress and her pets were toned down to suit the quiet situations of the play; but as the reading progressed, and the plot approached a climax, the antics of the group became so vigorous and drolly excited that my poor friend closed the MS. in despair, and abandoned himself to the unrestrained expression of his mirth, declaring that if he could write a play to equal the fun of Miss Terry and her cats, his fortune would be made."

Cowper loved his pet hares, spaniel, and cat, and wrote the well-known "Cat retired from business."

Gray wrote a poem on a cat drowned in a vase which contained gold-fish.

Cardinal Richelieu was a lover of the cat.

Montaigne had a favourite cat.

Among painters, Gottfried Mind was not only fond of cats, but was one of, if not the best at portraying them in action; and in England no one has surpassed Couldery in delineation, nor Miss Chaplin in perfection of modelling. I am the fortunate possessor of several of her models in terra cotta, which, though small, are beautiful in finish. Of one, Miss Chaplin informed me, the details were scratched in with a pin, for want of better and proper tools.

GAMES

CAT'S CRADLE OR CATCH CRADLE.

Dr. Brewer, in his "Dictionary of Phrase and Fable," thinks this "the corrupt for cratch cradle or manger cradle, in which the infant Saviour was laid. Cratch is the French *crêche* (a rack or manger), and to the present hour the racks which stand in the fields for cattle to eat from are called *cratches*." Of this, however, I am doubtful, though there is much reason in his suggestion. In Sussex and Kent, when I was a boy, it was commonly played among children, but always called cat's, *catch*, or scratch cradle, and consisted generally of two or more players. A piece of string, being tied at the ends, was placed on the fingers, and crossed and re-crossed to make a sort of cradle; the next player inserted his or her fingers, quickly taking it off; then the first catching it back, then the second again, then the first, as fast as possible, *catching* and taking off the string. Sometimes the sides were caught by the teeth of the players, one on each side, and as the hands were relaxed the faces were apart, then when drawn out it brought the faces together; the string being let go or not, and caught again as it receded, was according to the will of the players, the catching and letting go affording much merriment. When four or five played, the string rapidly passed from hand to hand until, in the rapidity of the motion, one missed, who then stood out, and so on until only one was left, winning the game of cat's, *catch*, or scratch cradle. It was varied also to single and double cradle, according to the number of crossings of the string. Catch is easily converted into *cat's*, or it might be so called from the *catching* or clawing at, to get and to hold, the entanglement.

CAT-TRAP, BAT, AND BALL.[L]

With the form of the trap our readers are, doubtless, acquainted; it will only be necessary for us to give the laws of the game. Two boundaries are equally placed at some distance from the trap, between which it is necessary for the ball to pass when struck by the batsman; if it fall outside either of them he loses his innings. Innings are drawn for, and the player who wins places the ball in the spoon of the trap, touches the trigger with the bat, and, as the ball ascends from the trap, strikes it as far as he can. One of the other players (who may be from two to half-a-dozen) endeavours to catch it. If he do so before it reaches the ground, or hops more than once, or if the striker miss the ball when he aims at it, or hits the trigger more than once without striking the ball, he loses his innings, and the next in order, which must previously be agreed on, takes his place. Should the ball be fairly struck, and not caught, as we have stated, the out-player, into whose hand it comes, bowls it from the place where he picks it up, at the trap, which if he hit, the striker is out; if he miss it the striker counts one towards the game, which may be any number decided on. There is also a practice in some places, when the bowler has sent in the ball, of the striker's guessing the number of bats' lengths it is from the trap; if he guess within the real number he reckons that number toward his game, but if he guess more than there really are he loses his innings. It is not necessary to make the game in one innings.

PUSS IN THE CORNER.[M]

This is a very simple, but, at the same time, a very lively and amusing game. It is played by five only; and the place chosen for the sport should be a square court or yard with four corners, or any place where there are four trees or posts, about equidistant from each other, and forming the four points of a square. Each of these points or corners is occupied by a player; the fifth, who is called Puss, stands in the centre. The game now commences; the players exchange corners in all directions; it is the object of the one who stands out to occupy any of the corners which may remain vacant for an instant during the exchanges. When he succeeds in so doing, that player who is left without a corner becomes the puss. It is to be observed, that if A and B attempt to exchange corners, and A gets to B's corner, but B fails to reach A's before the player who stands out gets there, it is B and not A who becomes Puss.

CAT AND MOUSE.

This is a French sport. The toys with which it is played consist of two flat bits of hard wood, the edges of one of which are notched. The game is played by two only; they are both blindfolded and tied to the ends of a long string, which is fastened in the centre to a post, by a loose knot, so as to play easily in the evolutions made by the players. The party who plays the mouse occasionally scrapes the toys together, and the other, who plays the cat, attracted by the sound, endeavours to catch him.

CAT AND MOUSE-HUNTING.

The game of "Hunt the Slipper" used frequently to be called "Cat and Mouse-hunting." It is generally played with a slipper, shoe, or even a piece of wood, which was called the mouse, the centre player being the cat, and trying to catch or find the mouse. The "Boy's Own Book" thus describes the game, but *not* as Cat and Mouse: "Several young persons sit on the ground in a circle, a slipper is given them, and one—who generally volunteers to accept the office in order to begin the game—stands in the centre, and whose business it is to 'chase the slipper by its sound.' The parties who are seated pass it round so as to prevent, if possible, its being found in the possession of any individual. In order that the player in the centre may know where the slipper is, it is occasionally tapped on the ground and then suddenly handed on to right or left. When the slipper is found in the possession of any one in the circle, by the player who is hunting it, the party on whom it is found takes the latter player's place."

TIP-CAT.

Is a game played with sticks of a certain length and a piece of wood sharpened off at each end, which is called the "cat." A ring is made on the ground with chalk, or the pointed part of the cat, which is then placed in the centre. One end being smartly struck by the player, it springs spinning upwards; as it rises it is again struck, and thus knocked to a considerable distance. It is played in two ways, one being for the antagonist to guess *how many sticks length* it is off the ring, which is measured, and if right he goes in; or he may elect to pitch the cat, if possible, into the ring, which if he succeeds in doing, he then has the pleasure of knocking the wood called the cat recklessly, he knows not whither, until it alights somewhere, on something or some one.

CAT I' THE HOLE. [N]

The name of a game well known in Fife, and perhaps in other counties. If seven boys are to play, six holes are made at certain distances. Each of the six stands at a hole, with a short stick in his hand; the seventh stands at a certain distance, holding a ball. When he gives the word, or makes the sign agreed upon, all the six must change holes, each running to his neighbour's hole, and putting his stick in the hole which he has newly seized. In making this change, the boy who has the ball tries to put it into the empty hole. If he succeeds in this, the boy who had not his stick (for the stick is the *cat*) in the hole for which he had run is put out, and must take the ball. When the *Cat* is *in the Hole*, it is against the laws of the game to put the ball into it.

NURSERY RHYMES AND STORIES

These are as plentiful as blackberries, and are far too numerous to be treated of here. Some are very old, such as "Puss in Boots," "Whittington and his Cat," "Hey, diddle, diddle!" etc. Some have a political meaning, others satirical, others amusing, funny, or instructive, while a few are unmeaning jangles. "Dame Trot and her Wonderful Cat," "The Cat and the Mouse," and, later, "The White Cat," "The Adventures of Miss Minette Cattina," are familiar to many of the present time. Of the older stories and rhymes there are enough to fill a book; not of or about the cat in particular, possibly; but even that—the old combined with those of modern date—might be done; and for such information and perusal the "Popular Rhymes," by J. O. Halliwell, will be found very interesting, space preventing the subject being amplified here. Nor do they come within the scope and intention for which I have written respecting the cat.

FISHING CATS

Having just come across a communication made to *The Kelso Mail*, in 1880, by a correspondent giving the signature of "March Brown," bearing on the subject to which I have already alluded ("Fishing Cats"), I deem it worthy of notice, corroborating, as it does, the statement so often made, and almost as often denied, that cats are adept fishers, not only for food, but likewise for the sport and pleasure they so derive. The writer says that "for several years it has been my happy fortune to fish the lovely Tweed for salmon and trout. From Tweed Well to Coldstream is a long stretch, but I have fished it all, and believe that though other rivers have their special advantages, there is not one in Britain which offers such varied and successful angling as the grand Border stream. Many have been the boatmen whom I have employed whilst fishing for salmon, and all were fairly honest, except in the matter of a little poaching. Some had the complaint more fiercely than others, and some so bad as to be incurable. One of the afflicted (Donald by name) was an excellent boatman by day; as to his nocturnal doings I deemed it best not to inquire, except on those occasions when he needed a holiday to attend a summons with which the police had favoured him. Now any one who has studied the proclivities of poachers, knows that they have wonderful powers over all animals who depend upon them, such as dogs, cats, ferrets, tame badgers, otters, etc., etc. Donald's special favourite was a lady-cat, which followed him in his frequent fishings, and took deep interest in the sport. Near to his cottage on the river-bank was a dam or weir, over which the water trickled here and there a few inches deep. In the evenings of spring and summer Donald was generally to be found fishing upon this favourite stretch with artificial fly for trout, and, being an adept in the art, he seldom fished in vain. Pretty puss always kept close behind him, watching the trail of the mimic flies till a fish was hooked, and then her eagerness and love of sport could not be controlled, and so soon as the captive was in shoal water, in sprang puss up to the shoulders, and, fixing her claws firmly in the fish, brought it to the bank, when, with a caress from Donald, she again took her place behind him till another trout was on the line, and the sport was repeated. In this way did puss and her master pass the evenings, each proud of the other's doings, and happy in their companionship. Such was the affection of the cat for her master, that she could not even bear to be separated from him by day. Donald had charge of a ferry across the river, and no sooner did a bell at the opposite side of the stream give notice that a passenger was ready to voyage across, than down scampered puss to the boat, and, leaping in, she journeyed with her master to the further side, and again returned, gravely watching each stroke of the oar. Many a voyage did she thus daily make, and I question, with these luxurious boatings and the exciting fishing in the evenings, if ever cat was more truly happy. The love of fishing once developed itself to the disturbance of my own sport. With careful prevision, my boatman had, in the floods of November and December, secured a plentiful supply of minnows, to be held in readiness till wanted in my fishings for salmon in the ensuing February and March. The minnows were placed in a well two or three feet deep, and the cold spring water rendered them as tough as angler could desire. All went well for the first few days of the salmon fishing; the minnows were deemed admirable for the purpose, and the supply ample for our needs; but this good fortune was not to last. One morning the boatman reported a serious diminution of stock in the well, and on the following day things were still worse. Suspicion fell on more than one honest person, and we determined to watch late and early till the real thief was discovered. When the guidwife and bairns were abed, the boatman kept watch from the cottage window, and by the aid of a bright moon the mystery was soon solved. At the well-side stood puss, the favourite of the household; with arched back and extended paw she took her prey. When an unfortunate minnow approached the surface, sharp was the dash made by puss, arm and shoulder were boldly immersed, and straightway the victim lay gasping on the bank. Fishing in this manner, she soon captured half-a-dozen, and was then driven away. From that evening the well was always covered with a net, which scared puss into enforced honesty. By nature cats love dry warmth and sunshine, whilst they hate water and cold. Who has not seen the misery of a cat when compelled to step into a shallow pool, and how she examines her wet paw with anxiety, holding it up as something to be pitied? And yet the passion of destructiveness is so strong within them as to overcome even their aversion to water."

The following still more extraordinary circumstance of a cat fishing in the sea, appeared in *The Plymouth Journal*, June, 1828: "There is now at the battery on the Devil's Point, a cat, which is an expert catcher of the finny tribe, being in the constant habit of diving into the sea, and bringing up the fish alive in her mouth, and depositing them in the guard-room for the use of the soldiers. She is now seven years old, and has long been a useful caterer. It is supposed that her pursuits of the water-rats first taught her to venture into the water, to which it is well known puss has a natural aversion. She is as fond of the water as a Newfoundland dog, and takes her regular peregrinations along the rocks at its edge, looking out for her prey, ready to dive for them at a moment's notice."

CATS AND HORSES

From time immemorial cats have been kept in stables, and when this is the case there is generally a friendly feeling between one or other of the horses and the cat or cats. Such I have known with the heavy, ponderous cart-horse and his feline companion; such was the case in my stable, and so in many others. Cats are as a rule fond of horses, and the feeling is generally reciprocated. Several of our "race winners" have had their favourites at home, among others the well-known "Foxhall." "Many famous horses have had their stable cats, and the great, amiable Foxhall has adopted a couple of kittens, if it would not be more correct to say that they have adopted him. A pretty little white and a tabby, own brothers, live in Foxhall's box, and when Hatcher, his attendant, has rubbed him over, and put on his clothing, he takes up the kittens from the corner of the box where they have been waiting, and gently throws them on Foxhall's back. They are quite accustomed to the process, and, catching hold, soon settle down and curl themselves up into little fluffy balls, much to their own satisfaction and to the good horse's likewise, to judge from the way in which he turns and watches the operation."

In Lawrence's "History of the Horse," it is stated that the celebrated Arabian stallion, Godolphin, and a black cat were for many years the warmest friends. When the horse died, in 1753, the cat sat upon his carcase till it was put under ground, and then, crawling slowly and reluctantly away, was never seen again till her dead body was found in a hay-loft. Stubbs painted the portraits of the Arabian and the cat. There was a hunter in the King's stables at Windsor, to which a cat was so attached, that whenever he was in the stable the creature would never leave her usual seat on the horse's back, and the horse was so well pleased with the attention that, to accommodate his friend, he slept, as horses will sometimes do, standing.

"GRAMMER'S CAT AND OURS "

BY JOHN TABOIS TREGELLAS.

John Tabois Tregellas (1792-1865), born at St. Agnes. The greatest master of the niceties of the Cornish dialect, in which he wrote largely, both in prose and verse. The piece quoted from is included in a volume of miscellanies published by Mr. Netherton, Truro, and happily indicates the marked difference between the modern dialect of Cornwall and that of Devon, illustrated in "Girt Ofvenders an' Zmal." The hero of "Grammer's Cat" was a miner named Jim Chegwidden.

To wash his hands and save the floshing,
　　Outside the door Jim did his washing,
But soon returned in haste and fright—
　　"Mother, aw come! and see the sight;
Up on our house there's such a row,
　　Millions of cats es up there now!"
Jim's mother stared, and well she might;
　　She knew that Jim had not said right.
"'Millions of cats,' you said; now worn't it so?"
　　"Why, iss," said Jim, "and I beleeve ut too;
Not millions p'rhaps, but thousands must be theere,
　　And fiercer cats than they you'll never hear;
They're spitting, yowling, and the fur is flying,
　　Some of 'em's dead, I s'pose, and some is dying;
Such dismal groans I'm sure you never heard,
　　Aw, mother! ef you ded, you'd be affeered."
"Not I," said Jinny; "no, not I, indeed;

A hundred cats out theere, thee'st never seed."
Said Jim, "I doan't knaw 'zackly to a cat,
　They must be laarge wauns, then, to do like that;
They maake such dismal noises when they're fighting,
　Such scrowling, and such tearing, and such biting."
"Count ev'ry cat," says Jinny, "'round and 'round;
　Iss, rams and yaws, theer caan't be twenty found."
"We'll caall 'em twenty, mother, ef 'twill do;
　Shut all the cats, say I; let's have my stew."
"No, Jimmy, no!—no stew to-night,'
　Tell all the cats es counted right."
"Heere goes," said Jim; "lev Grammer's cat go fust
　(Of all the thievish cats, he es the wust).
You knaw Mal Digry's cat, he's nither black nor blue,
　But howsomever, he's a cat, and that maakes two;
Theer's that theer short-tailed cat, and she's a he,
　Short tail or long now, mother, that maakes three;
Theer's that theer grayish cat what stawl the flour,
　Hee's theere, I s'pose, and that, you knaw, maakes fower;
Trevenen's black es theere, ef he's alive,
　Now, mother, doan't 'ee see, why, that maakes five;
That no-tailed cat, that wance was uncle Dick's,
　He's sure theere to-night, and that maakes six;
That tabby cat you gove to Georgey Bevan,
　I knaw *his* yowl—he's theere, and that maakes seven;
That sickly cat we had, cud ait no mait,
　She's up theere too to-night, and she maakes 'ight;
That genteel cat, you knaw, weth fur so fine,
　She's surely theere, I s'pose, and that maakes nine;
Tom Avery's cat es theere, they caall un Ben,
　A reg'lar fighter he, and he maakes ten;
The ould maid's cat, Miss Jinkin broft from Devon,
　I s'pose she's theere, and that, you knaw, maakes 'leven;
Theere's Grace Penrose's cat, got chets, 'tes awnly two,
　And they're too young to fight as yet; so they waan't do.

281

Iss, 'leven's all that I can mind,
　Not more than 'leven you waan't find;
So lev me have my supper, mother,
　And let the cats ait one another."
"No, Jimmy, no!It shaan't be so;
　No supper shu'st thou have this night
Until the cats thee'st counted right;
　Go taake the lantern from the shelf,
And go and count the cats thyself."
　See hungry Jimmy with his light,
Turned out to count the cats aright;
　And he who had Hugh Tonkin blamed
Did soon return, and, much ashamed,
　Confessed the number was but two,
And both were cats that well he knew
　.Jim scratched his head,And then he said—
"Theere's Grammer's cat and ours out theere,
And they two cats made all that rout theere;
　But ef two cats made such a row,
'Tes like a thousand, anyhow."

LOST

How beautiful she was in her superb calmness, so graceful, so mild, and yet so majestic! Ah! I was a younger man then, of course, than I am now, and possibly more impressionable; but I thought her then the most perfect creature I had ever beheld. And even now, looking back through the gathering mists of time and the chilling frosts of advancing age, and recalling what she was, I endorse that earlier sentiment—she lives in my memory now, as she lived in my presence then, as the most perfect creature I ever beheld.

I had gone the round of all the best boarding-houses in town, when, at last, I went to Mrs. Honeywold's, and there, in her small, unpretending establishment, I, General Leslie Auchester, having been subdued, I trust, to a proper and humble state of mind by my past experiences, agreed to take up my abode.

And it was there I first met her! Hers was the early maturity of loveliness, perfect in repose, with mild, thoughtful eyes, intelligent and tender, a trifle sad at times, but lighting up with quick brilliancy as some new object met her view, or some vivid thought darted its lightning flash through her brain—for she was wonderfully quick of perception—with an exquisite figure, splendidly symmetrical, yet swaying and supple as a young willow, and with unstudied grace in every quick, sinewy motion.

She spent little upon dress (I was sure she was not wealthy); but though there was little variety, her dress was always exquisitely neat and in perfect good taste, of some soft glossy fabric, smooth as silk and lustrous as satin, and of the softest shade of silver-gray, that colour so beautiful in itself, and so becoming to beautiful wearers; simply made, but fitting with a nicety more like the work of nature than of art to every curve and outline of that full and stately figure, and finished off round her white throat with something scarcely whiter.

She never wore ornaments of any kind, no chain, no brooch, no ring or pin. She had twins—two beautiful little blue-eyed things, wonderfully like herself—little shy, graceful creatures, always together, always playful. She never spoke of her own affairs, and affable as she was, and gentle in manner, there was something about her which repelled intrusion.

When, after some weeks' residence there, I had gained the good-will of my simple-minded but kindly little landlady, I cautiously ventured to ask her to gratify my not, I think, unnatural curiosity; but I found, to my surprise, she knew but little more than I did myself.

"She came to me," she said, "just at the edge of the evening, one cold rainy night, and I could not refuse to give her shelter, at least for the night, or till she could do better. I did not think of her remaining; but she is so pretty and gentle, and innocent-looking, I could not turn her out of my house—could I, now? I know I am silly in such ways; but what could I do?"

"But is it possible," I said, "that she has remained here ever since, and you know nothing more about her?"

"No more than you do yourself, general," said Mrs. Honeywold. "I do not even know where she lived before she came here. I cannot question her, and now, indeed, I have become so fond of her, I should not be willing to part with her; and I would not turn her and her little ones out of my house for the world!"

Further conversation elicited the fact that she was not a boarder, but that she and her little ones were the dependents upon Mrs. Honeywold's charity.

One fine summer day I had made an appointment with a friend to drive out to his place in the suburbs and dine with him, returning in the evening. When I came down in the afternoon, dressed for my excursion, I went into the dining-room to tell Mrs. Honeywold she need not wait for me. As I came back through the parlour, *she* was there alone. She was sitting on the sofa. A book lay near her, but I do not think she had been reading. She was sitting perfectly still, as if lost in reverie, and her eyes looked heavy with sleep or thought. But as I passed out of the room I looked back. I saw she had risen to her feet, and standing with her graceful figure drawn up to its full height, she was looking after me, with a look which I flattered myself was a look of interest. Ah, how well I remember that look!

The day had been a beautiful one, though sultry; but in the early evening we had a heavy thunder-shower, the violence of the summer rain delaying my return to town for an hour or two; and when the rain ceased, the evening was still starless, cloudy, and damp; and as I drove back to town I remember that the night air, although somewhat freshened by the rain, was warm, and heavy with the scent of unseen flowers.

It was late when I reached the quiet street where I had taken up my abode, and as I mounted the steps I involuntarily felt for my latch-key, but to my surprise I found the hall-door not only unfastened, but a little way opened.

"Why, how is this, Mrs. Honeywold?" I said, as my landlady met me in the hall. "Do you know that your street-door was left open?"

"Yes," she said, quietly, "I know it."

"But is it safe?" I asked, as I turned to lock the door; "and so late, too."

"I do not think there is any danger," she said. "I was on the watch; I was in the hall myself, waiting."

"Not waiting for me, I hope?" said I; "that was surely unnecessary."

"No, not for you," she answered. "I presume you can take care of yourself; but," she added, in a low voice, "she is out, and I was waiting to let her in."

"Out at this time of night!—that seems strange. Where has she gone?"

"I do not know."

"And how long has she been gone?" I asked, as I hung up my

hat.

"I cannot tell just what time she went out," she said; "I know she was in the garden with the little ones, and came in just before tea. After they had had their suppers and gone to bed I saw her in the parlour alone, and when I came into the room again she was gone, and she has not returned, and I—"

"Oh, then she went out before the rain, did she?"

"Yes, sir; some time before the rain."

"Oh, then that explains it; she was probably caught out by the rain, and took shelter somewhere, and has been persuaded to stay. There is nothing to be alarmed at; you had better not wait up another moment."

"But I don't like to shut her out, general; I should not sleep a wink."

"Nonsense, nonsense!" I said. "Go to bed, you silly woman; you will hear her when she comes, of course, and can come down and let her in." And so saying, I retired to my own room.

The next morning at breakfast, I noticed that my landlady was looking pale and troubled, and I felt sure she had spent a sleepless night.

"Well, Mrs. Honeywold," I said, with assumed cheerfulness, as she handed my coffee to me, "how long did you have to sit up? What time did she come in?"

"She did not come in all night, general," said my landlady, in a troubled voice. "She has not come home yet, and I am very anxious about it."

"No need of that, I trust," I said, reassuringly; "she will come this morning, no doubt."

"I don't know. I wish I was sure of that. I don't know what to make of it. I don't understand it. She never did so before. How she could have stayed out, and left those two blessed little things all night—and she always seemed such a tender, loving mother, too—I don't understand it."

When I returned at dinner-time I found matters still worse. She had not returned. My poor landlady was almost in hysterics, though she tried hard to control herself.

To satisfy her I set off to consult the police. My mission was not encouraging. They promised to do their best, but gave slight hopes of a successful result.

So sad, weary, and discouraged, I returned home, only to learn there were no tidings of the missing one.

"I give her up now," said my weeping landlady; "I shall never see her again. She is lost for ever; and those two poor pretty little creatures—"

"By the way," I said, "I wanted to speak to you about them. If she never does return, what do you purpose to do with them?"

"Keep them!" said the generous and impulsive little woman.

"I wanted to say, if she does not return, I will, if you like, relieve you of one of them. My sister, who lives with me, and keeps my house, is a very kind, tender-hearted woman. There are no children in the house, and she would, I am sure, be very kind to the poor little thing. What do you say?"

"No, no!" sobbed the poor woman; "I cannot part with them. I am a poor woman, it is true, but not too poor to give them a home; and while I have a bit and a sup for myself they shall have one too. Their poor mother left them here, and if she ever does return she shall find them here. And if she never returns, then—"

And she never did return, and no tidings of her fate ever reached us. If she was enticed away by artful blandishments, or kidnapped by cruel violence, we knew not. But I honestly believe the latter. Either way, it was her fatal beauty that led her to destruction; for, as I have said before, she was the most perfect creature, the most beautiful Maltese cat, that I ever beheld in my life! I am sure she never deserted her two pretty little kittens of her own accord. And if—poor dumb thing—she was stolen and killed for her beautiful fur, still I say, as I said at first, she was "more sinned against than sinning."

—*C. H. Grattan, in Tit-Bits.*

FOOTNOTES:

[A]"Trans. Tyneside Nat. Field Club," 1864, vol. vi. p. 123.

[B]A lugged bear is a bear with its ears cut off, so that when used for baiting there is less hold for the dogs.

[C]Hone's "Every-day Book," vol. i.

[D]Mr. T. F. Thiselton Dyer's "English Folk-lore."

[E]Mr. T. F. Thiselton Dyer's "English Folk-lore."

[F]Harland and Wilkinson, "Lancashire Folk-lore," p. 141.

[G]Edwards's "Old English Customs," p. 54.

[H]Daniel's "Rural Sports," 1813.

[I]Hone's "Every-day Book," vol. i.

[J]Daniel's "Rural Sports," 1813.

[K]Daniel's "Rural Sports," 1813.

[L]The Boy's Own Book.

[M]The Boy's Own Book.

[N]Jamieson's "Scottish Dictionary."

Lightning Source UK Ltd.
Milton Keynes UK
UKHW012230291122
413043UK00005B/1071